BusinessWeek

The Insider's Guide to Mutual Funds

McGraw-Hill, Inc.

New York San Francisco Washington, D.C. Auckland Bogota
Caracas Lisbon London Madrid Mexico City Milan
Montreal New Delhi San Juan Singapore Sydney Tokyo Toronto

Library of Congress Cataloging-in-Publication Data
Business Week
The Insider's Guide to Mutual Funds
128 p. 28 cm.

ISBN 0-07-036016-2
1. Business. 2. Investing. 3. Reference
95-75703 CIP 1995

This book is printed on recycled, acid-free paper containing a minimum of 50% recycled, de-inked fiber.

Designed by Affinity Publishing, Inc. and Frank Loose Design

Front Cover Photograph: Comstock, Inc.
Back Cover Photograph: Comstock, Inc.
Illustration and Photo Credits: page 122

1 2 3 4 5 6 7 8 9 10-XX-98 97 96 95 94

Table of Contents

Preface

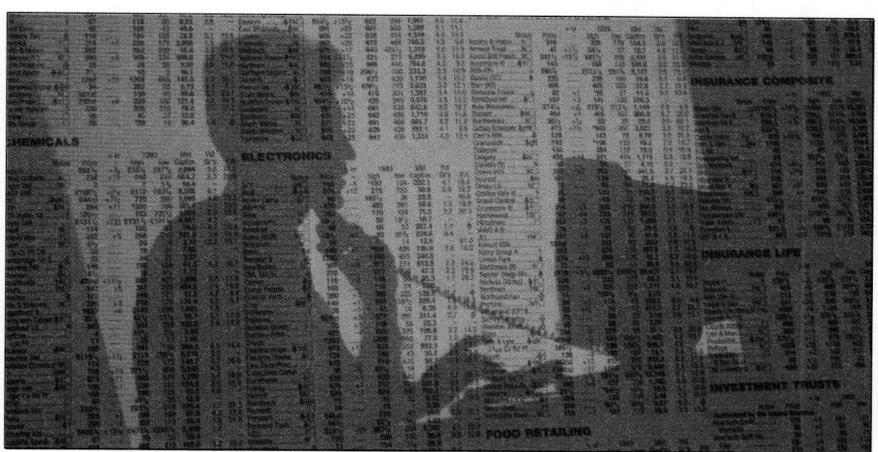

Over the last decade, mutual fund assets have grown over fivefold! Not surprisingly, *Business Week*'s annual Mutual Fund Scoreboard issue, *The Best Mutual Funds*, is continually a best seller. In fact, mutual fund executives think so highly about this special edition that they've given the last issue an "A-" rating, the highest among the seven publications surveyed.

Now the magazine with the best mutual fund scoreboard is proud to bring you *The Insider's Guide to Mutual Funds*. It's your passport to mutual fund investing. We provide you with all the information you need about mutual funds—what they are, how to use them to pursue your investment goals, how to buy and sell, and much more.

The first chapter is an introduction to the world of mutual funds: why they're popular and how to harness their earning power. Chapters 2–5 take a close-up look at the different types of funds—equity funds, bond funds, money-market, international funds, closed-end funds, convertible funds, and more.

In chapter 6 we explain how to buy and sell mutual funds, including details about commissions, or "loads", and the subtleties of front-end loads, back-end loads, low loads, hidden loads, and no loads.

Chapter 7 tells you how to build an investment portfolio of mutual funds. Then, to provide assistance once you have acquired your funds, chapter 8 discusses how to monitor them, to make sure you are making the most of your investments.

If you've made the right moves, you're making money. And if you're making money, you'll probably owe taxes. Chapter 9 explains the special tax rules that apply to mutual fund investors. We discuss how you can minimize the tax bite when cashing in your gains, and how to make the most of any unfortunate losses.

In short, *The Insider's Guide to Mutual Funds* answers your mutual fund questions and provides you with a roadmap to understanding and investing.

Chapter 1

Mutual Funds: The People's Choice

In recent years, American investors have embraced mutual funds with a fervor no one could have predicted. Since 1991, investors just like you have poured more than half a trillion dollars into stock and bond mutual funds.

At first, many financial market commentators and publications viewed this passion for mutual funds as a sure sign that the stock and bond markets were about to plunge. But they were wrong. The shift to mutual funds in the 1990s was caused by the historic drop in interest rates. The expected return from stocks is about 10 percent a year, more than three times the low-level returns reached in the early part of the 1990s from a CD or money-market fund. Investors correctly recognized that their long-term money (cash they could probably leave invested for at least 6 to 12 months) would do better in stock and bond funds. In a recent year, for example, the average equity fund was up 20 percent; the average bond fund, 11.7 percent. If you had been savvy or fortunate enough to invest in some of the top performers, the returns would have been startling. The twenty-five top equity funds recently delivered a 65 percent or better annual return, and the twenty-five top bond funds, better than 20 percent.

Novice investors will learn through experience that markets—and mutual fund prices—don't always go up. But investors who took a longer-term view have been rewarded for taking the small extra risk of mutual funds. In a low-interest-rate, low-inflation environment, the greater risk can be playing it too safe. Investors who keep their long-term funds in CDs and U.S. Treasury bills risk falling short of their long-term financial objectives, such as college educations for their children or comfortable retirements for themselves.

During the early 1990s, many mutual fund investors were, and are, first-timers. According to a recent survey by the Investment Company Institute, the mutual funds' trade association, 1 out of every 10 mutual fund investors first bought in during the previous two years. Some are older investors, who shifted a portion of their money out of banks in search of better returns. Many of the new investors, however, are baby-boomers. Mutual funds offer them a much more diverse and potentially rewarding menu of products than banks do. In fact, banks are selling mutual funds themselves. According to George Salem, a bank stock analyst for Prudential Securities, "mutual funds are the bank deposits of the 1990s." Notice, however, that unlike bank deposits, mutual fund investments are not insured.

While many investors are new to mutual funds, mutual funds are hardly new to many investors. They've been a fixture in the investment world since the 1920s. At first, funds offered mainly one sort of investment: stocks. Bond funds were few, and tax-free mutual funds didn't exist until the 1970s.

Because so many individuals have put so many dollars in the hands of mutual fund managers, mutual funds are today's largest and most active investors. Their needs and preferences set the tone for much of the market. Mutual funds also perform a critical function for the equity markets, using money from investors to finance emerging growth companies, which in turn create vast numbers of new jobs to help keep our economy strong.

Mutual funds are also the main buyers of municipal bonds. State and local governments increasingly turn to mutual funds to finance public services and infrastructure. The funds help governments save billions in interest expense.

The Explosive Growth in Mutual Funds

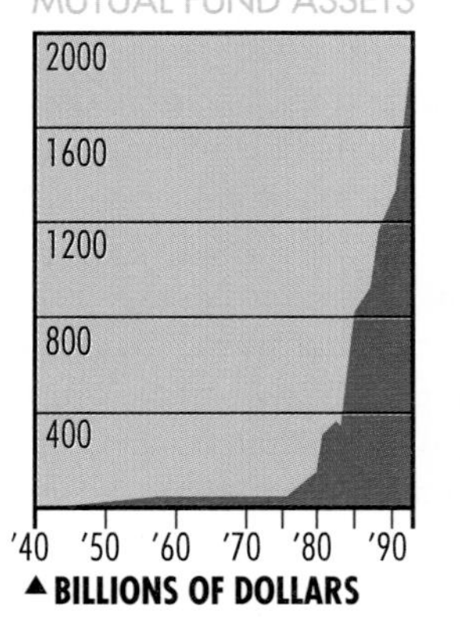

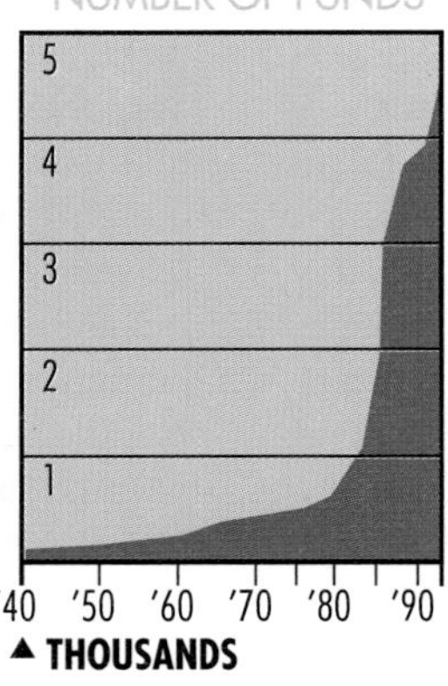

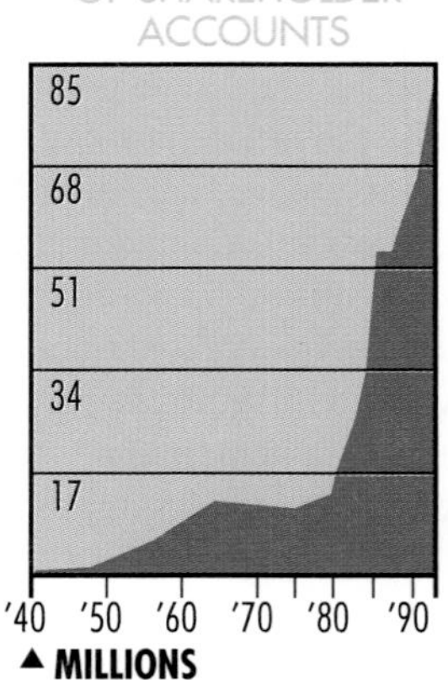

Mutual funds are key players in other markets, too. Through investment in U.S. Treasury securities, mutual funds help finance the budget deficit. Funds bring fresh capital to the home mortgage market through their purchases of mortgage-backed securities, making it easier and a little cheaper for families to buy homes. With investments in high-yield bonds and commercial paper, mutual funds are helping to reduce borrowing costs for corporations.

Over the last decade, fund companies have also developed "sector funds," which invest in a particular industry or group of industries. Such investment vehicles are designed to appeal to investors who might otherwise invest in individual stocks.

The growth of the mutual fund industry has even surprised industry officials. In 1990, for instance, an industry-sponsored study estimated that the funds would control $2 trillion in assets by 1995 or 1996, and at least $3 trillion by the year 2000. But the funds easily surpassed these predictions, and now by the estimated year, experts suggest that individuals may well have more money in mutual funds than in bank savings accounts and CDs. Since 1990, the number of funds has increased 24 percent to 4,558; the number of shareholder accounts more than doubled to 83 million.

This popularity is not simply a bull market phenomenon. Fund investors could just buy stocks and bonds directly but prefer the convenient and efficient funds as avenues to a splendid array of opportunities—from expensive blue-chip companies like Exxon, General Electric, and Philip Morris, to complex and difficult foreign markets, to fixed-income investing.

Make no mistake. Most mutual funds are riskier than bank deposits. No one guarantees your assets will remain intact, let alone grow. The only funds considered as safe as bank deposits are those investing solely in U.S. Treasury bills.

Table 1.1

The Biggest Mistakes of Fund Investors

- Buying last year's or last quarter's hottest performer only because it did so well.
- Ignoring the prospectus—especially the parts on fees and investment policy.
- Choosing funds inappropriate for investment goals.
- Selecting highest yields without regard for risks.
- Losing track of fund performance.
- Failure to keep records for investment evaluation and taxes.

Generally, funds are best for money you won't need in the near future. In fact, the longer your time horizon, the lower the risk of losses in mutual funds.

How do you find the right funds? *Business Week's Making Money with Mutual Funds* makes it easy. Whether you invest on your own or rely on the advice of a broker or financial planner, you'll do better with a solid grasp of mutual funds. If you enter the world of mutual funds as an educated consumer and avoid the common mistakes (see table 1.1), you have a good chance of becoming successful.

What Is a Mutual Fund?

A mutual fund is an investment company that pools the money of many individual investors. Your money buys shares of stock in the mutual fund itself. The fund uses this money to buy shares of another company's stocks, bonds, or other assets. The price of a mutual fund share reflects its total net value—the fund's assets less its liabilities—divided by the number of shares outstanding. This figure is also called the fund's net asset value, commonly referred to as "NAV."

Unlike stocks, whose prices are subject to change at each trade, mutual fund NAVs are calculated only at the close of each day's trading. To figure their NAVs, the funds use the closing prices of each security they own. (Bonds trade infrequently, so bond funds employ outside services to estimate their bonds' day-to-day prices.)

Who Should Invest in Mutual Funds?

Most mutual funds are organized to be "open-ended"—that is, the funds can issue an unlimited number of new shares as they take in money, and redeem any number of shares for cash as investors withdraw. A smaller number of funds are "closed-ended." They raise their capital only during offering periods. Once they close, they issue and redeem no further shares. Investors must trade their shares at a variable market price on a stock exchange, just like ordinary shares are traded.

Open-end and closed-end funds are both highly regulated by the Investment Company Act of 1940. Although regulators don't dictate investment policy, they do make sure investment managers adhere to prescribed standards of disclosure, record keeping, and administration. For the most part, the mutual funds have a fairly clean record. (In early 1994, Invesco Funds dismissed John Kaweske, one of its star portfolio managers, for allegedly failing to properly report his personal investments to management. It was later revealed that Kaweske was a director of a small biotech company in which he and his funds had stakes. Invesco claimed it never knew about his directorship, but Kaweske's lawyer said otherwise. None of this in itself was illegal, but the rules about what mutual fund managers can do with their own investments are meant to protect shareholders and the integrity of the funds. The Kaweske affair made all fund companies reconsider disclosure rules for employees, and no doubt sent regulators looking for violations.

Mutual funds are especially good for investors just getting started. If you have only $1,000 or $2,000 to invest, very few stockbrokers or professional money managers will bother with you. Those who do won't give you the attention and research support they offer their well-heeled clients—nor should you expect it. These stockbrokers and money managers must earn a living, and the commissions on your small account won't pay for much of their time.

Put the same money into a mutual fund, however, and some first-string portfolio managers *will* be working for you—and working hard. That's because the fund's performance is the manager's calling card. Its successes are chronicled in the media—and so are its failures. Such attention is a powerful incentive for the portfolio manager to give the fund his or her very best efforts.

What's more, the $1,000 investor gets the same proportional results as the $100,000 investor. That's why many investors who could afford their own stockbrokers and professional money managers actually prefer mutual funds. So do many institutional investors, including corporate pension plans and bank trust departments.

Service, convenience, and efficiency all help to explain the growth of mutual funds. But no one would invest in mutual funds if they didn't make money, which they have done plentifully for those wise enough to invest in them.

A New Generation of Fund Investors

Many of today's investors first encountered a mutual fund when they bought a money-market fund. In the late 1970s and early 1980s, the interest rates that banks and thrifts could pay savers were set by bank regulators and were kept artificially low. Those with $10,000 could buy Treasury bills, but there was no high-interest vehicle for individuals with less money—that is, until money-market mutual funds revolutionized savings in America. They pooled investors' money and bought the higher-yielding money-market investments that individuals could not get on their own. Now, when short-term interest rates soar, money-market funds allow anyone to reap the benefits.

Later, when the great bull market in stocks and bonds got under way during the 1980s, mutual funds attracted millions of new customers and on average earned for them an annual total return of 14.9 percent. A $1,000 investment in the average equity fund at the start of the decade would have grown to slightly over $4,000 by the decade's end.

More recently, the tide seems to have shifted toward small- to medium-sized companies which many fund analysts think can continue to beat the S&P companies for years to come. Such a prediction indeed bodes well for mutual fund performance.

One academic study pondered the question, "Do winners repeat?" The academics examined monthly mutual fund returns during the period from 1976 to 1988 and concluded that a review of past performance is useful in differentiating one mutual fund from another. Although it's not wise to continually switch into the No. 1 performing fund from the previous period, it is advisable to invest in funds that remain among the best year after year.

The Joys of Compound Growth

If you're ever cornered by an investment salesperson, he or she will eventually whip out a typical "mountain" chart, which depicts the growth of a onetime investment under the influence of steady improvement and compound interest. The line rises slowly at first but soon accelerates and appears to jump off the page.

Sales hype? Well, such track records are real. Templeton Growth Fund, one of the first funds that invested in non–U.S. stocks, has an average annual return of 14.8 percent over some 40 years. An original $10,000 investment four decades ago would be worth nearly $500,000 today. With reinvestment of dividends and capital gains, the total value would be almost $2.2 million!

Table 1.2

The Wonderful World of Compound Interest

INVEST $10,000 IN YEAR 1

What your investment would be worth at the end of . . .

Rate of Return	5 years	10 years	15 years	20 years	25 years	30 years
7%	$ 14,026	$ 19,672	$ 27,950	$ 38,697	$ 54,274	$ 76,123
8%	14,693	21,589	31,722	46,610	68,485	100,627
9%	15,386	23,674	36,425	56,044	86,231	132,677
10%	16,105	25,937	41,772	67,275	108,347	174,494
11%	16,851	28,394	47,846	80,623	135,855	228,923
12%	17,623	31,058	54,736	96,463	170,001	299,599

INVEST $2,000 EVERY YEAR

What your investment would be worth at the end of . . .

Rate of Return	5 years	10 years	15 years	20 years	25 years	30 years
7%	$ 12,307	$ 29,567	$ 53,776	$ 87,730	$ 135,353	$ 202,146
8%	12,672	31,291	58,649	98,846	157,909	244,692
9%	13,047	33,121	64,007	111,529	184,648	297,150
10%	13,431	35,062	69,899	126,005	216,364	361,887
11%	13,826	37,123	76,380	142,530	253,998	441,826
12%	14,230	39,309	83,507	161,398	298,668	540,585

INVEST $200 PER MONTH

What your investment would be worth at the end of . . .

Rate of Return	5 years	10 years	15 years	20 years	25 years	30 years
7%	$ 14,402	$ 34,819	$ 63,762	$ 104,793	$162,959	$245,417
8%	14,793	36,833	69,669	118,589	191,473	300,059
9%	15,198	38,993	76,249	134,579	225,906	368,895
10%	15,616	41,310	83,585	153,139	267,578	455,865
11%	16,049	43,797	91,772	174,715	318,116	566,046
12%	16,497	46,468	100,915	199,830	379,527	705,983

But the same principle applies to a compound-interest investment in any mutual fund. If you leave the interest and dividends to grow, the results can be remarkable.

Look at table 1.2. If you invest $10,000 now, reinvest your returns over 20 years, and earn 11 percent on average, your nest egg grows more than eightfold—to $80,623. An 11 percent return on $10,000 is $1,100. Over 20 years, that totals $22,000. So, after two decades, your $10,000 initial investment and the annual return on it account for $32,000. The extra $48,000 is the benefit of compounding—a return on your returns.

Of course, mutual funds rarely guarantee any rate of return. The portfolio managers simply do their best to deliver the highest rate of return they can within their investment restrictions and objectives. What's more, a fund averaging 11 percent a year earns more in some years, less in others. Only in retrospect is the return steady and predictable.

Nevertheless, if you want to harness the power of compound rates of return, investing in mutual funds is a convenient and efficient way to do it. Suppose, for example, that you own some bonds and collect $389 in interest twice a year. You want to reinvest the money but you can't buy more bonds, because it's an odd amount. With a bond mutual fund, however, any dividend can be immediately reinvested through the fund in the same types of bonds you already own. You don't have to worry about odd amounts of money, checks delayed in the mail, or temporarily idle funds. The mutual fund divides your dividend by its current price per share and then credits you with that many additional shares. If it works out to 17.693 shares, no problem.

This freedom to invest odd sums and buy fractional shares makes

A knowledgeable broker can explain the many finer points of investing.

mutual funds ideal for savings programs. Millions of investors, in fact, have automatic investment plans helping them compound their money.

Suppose you want to invest $200 a month in equities. It's not practical to buy $200 worth of stock at a time. Commissions would be high, and there's no way to invest odd amounts or buy fractional shares of stock. But there's no problem doing this within a mutual fund. As you can see in table 1.2, a regular savings program invests new money in the fund at more frequent intervals, making compound growth work even faster.

Be Realistic about Your Expectations

Remember the mythical investor whose $10,000 investment eventually made him a millionaire? Notice that he didn't become a millionaire instantaneously. Starting with $10,000, even 20 percent a year will take you 26 years to reach one million dollars. Mutual funds won't get you rich quick, but if you persist in investing and select funds that are consistently good, your wealth will certainly grow.

Whatever funds you choose, be realistic. Mutual funds invest in specific kinds of security or particular markets. If you choose an equity fund that invests in large capitalization stocks, your hope is that it's going to perform better than the S&P 500. But if the S&P goes down 20 percent, it's unrealistic to expect your fund to go up. Likewise, if you're investing in a money-market fund when Treasury bill rates are 6 percent, don't expect a 10 percent return.

As an investor, you have no control over the market—but you *do* have control over your portfolio. It's difficult to buy and sell funds just to catch the ups and avoid the downs of the market, known as "market-timing" (see chapter 7 for more on this). But it's easy to select funds carefully, monitor their performance, keep investments matched to your financial objectives, and reap the rewards of a long-term investment program.

Chapter 2

Equity Funds

At one time, mutual funds primarily invested in large U.S. corporations. Today, however, funds specialize in everything from biotechnology to small Asian companies to municipal bonds issued within a single state. Funds are so numerous and varied that investors would be overwhelmed without some method in which to organize the offerings. This chapter will help you get a sense of one part of the world of mutual funds—the "stock" or equity funds, and how they invest your money. Other chapters that follow will cover other varieties of mutual funds.

Equity funds are simply those that invest in equities, or common stocks. Many of the companies most widely held by equity funds are household names (see table 2.1). Examine the column "Percentage of Net Assets." The FNMA (Federal National Mortgage Association), known as "Fannie Mae," is the stock most commonly found in mutual fund portfolios, but it amounts to only slightly more than six-tenths of 1 percent of the net assets of all equity mutual fund holdings. Each of the

Table 2.1

Equity Mutual Funds

LARGEST HOLDINGS

Stock	Percentage of Net Assets
FNMA (Fannie Mae)	0.61%
General Electric	0.56
AT&T	0.55
Motorola	0.52
Intel	0.51
GTE	0.42
MCI Communications	0.38
Philip Morris	0.37
Chrysler	0.36
BankAmerica	0.36
Exxon	0.36
Texaco	0.33
Citicorp	0.33
E. I. Dupont de Nemours	0.31
American Express	0.31
Bristol-Myers Squibb	0.31
Sears Roebuck	0.31
Time Warner	0.31
General Motors	0.30
Ford Motor	0.29
Mobil	0.29
Eastman Kodak	0.28
Wal-Mart Stores	0.28
Xerox	0.28
Pfizer	0.28

next four largest holdings makes up only a little more than half a percent of equity fund assets. Altogether, the 25 largest holdings only amount to little more than 9 percent of equity funds' net assets. That shows the general pattern of diversified fund portfolios.

Specific funds are diversified or concentrated to meet different goals. Some mutual funds, for example, invest for "maximum growth," or for "growth," or for "income." Others go for specific markets or technologies. They all try to make you money, but they do it in different ways.

Bond funds are also extremely varied. Some buy high-yield—or "junk"—bonds, others invest in tax-exempt municipal bonds, and still others in foreign bonds. (Bond funds will be discussed at length in chapter 3.)

Looking at funds based on their objectives is part of the investment process. You learn about how they behave and what returns you can expect. Then you compare this to the kind of investor you are and the goals you are trying to achieve.

Types of Equity Funds

Maximum-Growth Funds

Remember the nursery rhyme about the "pretty little girl" with the curl on her forehead? That describes the behavior of "maximum-growth" mutual funds: When they're good, they're very, very good, and when they're bad, they're horrid.

A fund can score a 96 percent gain in one year—more than half of it in the first quarter—but a year earlier or later, it can deliver one of the worst performances around, losing 30 percent or more in an equivalent period. Maximum-growth funds often score near the top—or the bottom—of the heap, as share prices fluctuate wildly. Some investors use the term "aggressive growth" for these funds, which are best suited to investors with the time and patience to wait for the big payoffs.

One reason these funds carry high risk is because they frequently invest in smaller, less mature companies, including many initial public offerings (stock offered for sale to the public for the first time). Such companies are usually growing quickly and trade at high prices relative to their earnings per share. Some have no earnings at all and may have no actual products to sell, yet they spend heavily on research and development. The prices of these stocks often reflect a rosy outlook for the company, and prices can plummet if bad news or poor financial results suddenly cloud the forecast. Furthermore, such companies usually don't pay dividends, so the main source of profits for the growth fund that owns them is rising stock prices. Often the most successful of these funds are small. As success helps make them larger, their performance can easily become less dynamic.

The portfolios of maximum-growth funds often include such cutting-edge industries as biotechnology, computers, software, or medical technology. These companies may go years without profits. That's why some funds are labeled "emerging growth."

Some emerging-growth issues are "concept" or "story" stocks, where the shares have appeal not on the basis of current earnings, but on the credibility of the "story" that promises great profits. Among the faddish concepts on Wall Street is "interactive multimedia" or the "information highway"—a still hazy melding of entertainment, telecommunications, cable television, software, and computer hardware that will bring 500 channels of television to your home and office. Multimedia is not intended solely for couch potatoes but instead is intended to allow viewers to "interact" as well. Several of the largest holdings in maximum-growth funds are major multimedia "story" stocks.

In recent years, some maximum-growth funds have begun concentrating their portfolios in a few industries, or using various forms of leverage—margin, options, or futures—to maximize returns. With this approach, maximum-growth funds may invest in more predictable companies like Nabors Industries, an oilfield equipment maker, and Home Depot, the giant home improvement retailer.

Other maximum-growth funds—such as American Heritage, AIM Constellation, Dreyfus Capital Growth, Dreyfus Strategic Growth, and Kaufmann—are selling stocks short. In a short sale, the portfolio manager borrows stock through a broker, sells the stock, and pockets the proceeds. Later, the portfolio manager will have to buy enough stock at the prevailing price to replace the borrowed shares. If the short-seller is right, the stock can be replaced on the cheap. The difference between the higher sales price and the lower purchase price is the short-seller's profit.

In effect, short-selling merely reverses the usual "buy low, sell high" chronology; instead, it's "sell high, buy low." But it's riskier than buying stocks before you sell them—and here's why: When you purchase a $10 stock, your worst loss could be $10 a share. After you sell short, however, the stock price can continue to climb. While a stock buyer has unlimited upside potential, a short-seller has potential for unlimited losses.

Because maximum-growth funds make riskier investments than other funds, you would expect them to deliver the maximum returns in bull markets and fare the worst in bear markets.

Within the maximum-growth category, almost anything goes as long as the fund manager thinks he or she can make money for the shareholders by investing in it. If you can stand the risk, these funds can be very rewarding, but those who buy them should pay extra attention to what's happening in the market and in these portfolios. They're definitely not for buy-and-forget investors.

Small-Company Funds

Because maximum-growth funds often invest in the stocks of small companies, you might consider them small-company funds. Sometimes, however, there's not much difference between the two types of mutual fund portfolios.

Small-company funds are big buyers of IPOs, for example, but not all small-company funds are aggressive, nor do they invest in high-risk or high-tech businesses. Many invest in mundane businesses like auto parts, home building, and savings and loans. Others build top performance with both high-tech and low-tech businesses—for example, retailers, food companies, and financial services.

Many investment pros say a small company stock is one with a market capitalization—that is, the number of shares multiplied by the price per share—of less than $1 billion. That may sound like a lot of money, but remember that Exxon has a market capitalization of more than $75 billion.

The Babson Enterprise Fund hunts for opportunities in stocks in the $15 million to $300 million market cap range, while Babson Enterprise II works between $250 million and $1 billion. Other small-company funds look to invest in companies with less than $250 million in sales or buy only stocks sold over the counter (OTC).

While some small-company funds get rid of their holdings in companies that grow too large, many don't. Instead, they keep them as long as they remain good investments. This explains why companies like Intel (market capitalization: $25 billion) and Oracle Systems (market capitalization: $9 billion) are still held by some small-company funds (see table 2.2).

Table 2.2

Small-Company Funds

LARGEST HOLDINGS

Stock	Percentage of Net Assets
International Game Technology	1.11%
Cisco Systems	1.09
Oracle Systems	0.87
Intel	0.73
Synoptics Communications	0.72
Newbridge Networks	0.65
Sybase	0.57
DSC Communications	0.55
Electronic Arts	0.54
Medco Containment Services	0.52

The rationale for investing in small companies is simple. Because they start from a smaller base, they often grow much faster than large companies. A new product or service that might not even be noticed on the bottom line at a large multinational can swell a small company's coffers. Growth in revenues, profits, and book value is what drives the stock prices.

Cisco Systems, Inc., the small-company funds' No. 2 holding, manufactures the hardware needed to connect computers into networks. It first sold stock to the public in early 1990 when revenues were about $28 million, profits about $4.2 million, and the stock price as low as $2.25 a share (adjusted for stock splits). Within three years, annual revenues were over $800 million, profits over $190 million, and the stock sold at $58.

Not every small company grows like Cisco, however. That's why investing in new companies is best left to professionals, and why small-company funds don't consistently perform well.

Still, the long-term case for investing in small companies is compelling. Over the last six decades small-company stocks earned a 12.2 percent average annual return versus 10.3 percent for the S&P 500. Don't minimize the impact of the 1.9 percentage-point differential. If your $10,000 investment earns 10.3 percent over 20 years, your nest egg grows to $71,000. At 12.2 percent, it's only a shade under $100,000!

Small-company funds attracted a great deal of attention in the early 1990s. During one three-year period, their average return was more than twice that of the S&P 500. However, small-company funds that are too successful can undermine their own future. As small funds investing in small companies, they can be nimble and quick. A $25 million small-company fund may have no difficulty finding small-company stocks at attractive prices. Once it has $100 million to invest, however, it may find fewer good selections, and investing new money in the old winners means buying at higher prices.

For this reason, some successful small-company funds refuse new money. In recent years, FAM Value, John Hancock Special Equities, Monetta, Mutual Discovery, Strong Common Stock, and T. Rowe Price Small-Cap Value all shut their doors to new investors, although existing shareholders can add to their accounts.

If you're locked out of some small-company funds, look for others. With the multitude of small-company stocks emerging, there are no shortage of suitable funds to invest in. Many stock market pros now expect small stocks to outpace the larger ones for years to come. One reason is that large institutional investors are beginning to invest more heavily in smaller companies. In addition, well-managed small companies might have an edge in today's slow-growth economy. After all, it's easier for a company with $100 million in sales to double its revenues than it is for a $10 billion one.

But choosing the right small-company fund is critical. Since small companies are far more diverse—there are more than 5,000 stocks out there but only 10 percent or so can be considered "large"—the fund manager's stock selection can leave the fund way out of the money.

To eliminate some of this risk, you might invest in small companies through an index fund such as the Vanguard Index Small Capitalization Stock Fund, which replicates the Russell 2000 index, a broad measure of the small-company universe. Most likely, it will never be the No. 1 fund. Yet, in a recent year, the fund was up 18.7 percent—27th out of 75 comparable funds. In this very competitive marketplace, you *could* do worse!

Table 2.3

Growth Funds

LARGEST HOLDINGS

Stock	Percentage of Net Assets
FNMA (Fannie Mae)	1.27%
Motorola	1.20
Intel	1.10
Chrysler	0.87
MCI Communications	0.72
AT&T	0.61
Microsoft	0.61
Time Warner	0.60
Home Depot	0.60
Wal-Mart Stores	0.59

Growth Funds

Long-term investors like growth funds, which generally search for stocks with the best capital appreciation potential, leaving dividend income a secondary consideration. America's best-known mutual fund and largest equity fund, the $31.7 billion Fidelity Magellan Fund, is a growth fund. Most mutual fund companies have several types of growth funds.

In its simplest form, growth stock investing is choosing companies whose revenues and earnings are accelerating. Even if you're not a stock market maven, you'd recognize many of the largest holdings of these funds as listed in table 2.3.

Although investing in growth companies makes good sense, it isn't always the most rewarding strategy. Growth stocks go in and out of favor on Wall Street, and the growth funds' performance reflects that.

Although all growth funds profess common goals, their approaches vary. Twentieth Century's growth funds, for instance, stay "fully invested"—that is, every dollar is used to buy stocks. The Janus Fund, in contrast, keeps a large cash reserve and waits for the right opportunities. The Mathers Fund will even drop almost all its equity investments if necessary. During a recent three-year period, it held very few stocks—and the results show it, averaging 4.8 percent per year versus 20.1 percent for the average U.S. diversified fund.

Not all growth funds invest in what most of us would consider growth stocks. Among the largest holdings of the T. Rowe Price Capital Appreciation Fund, for example, are Monsanto, a major chemical company; Polaroid, the photography firm; and Overseas Shipholding Group—stocks which are considered "value" rather than growth stocks.

Value Funds

The value funds eschew a company's earnings and try to buy "intrinsic value." Companies favored by value funds may have an undistinguished earnings record because they are companies in cyclical industries linked to the ups and downs of the business cycle—like chemicals, steel, aluminum, auto, or construction. Value funds try to buy these stocks when they're near the bottom of their cycle.

The auto industry is favored by value fund investors due to its cyclical nature.

Value investors may entirely disregard earnings potential to seek companies that possess prized assets or franchises, such as real estate, brand names, or broadcasting licenses.

Mutual Shares (and its sister funds Mutual Qualified, Mutual Beacon, and Mutual Discovery) apply the value concept to bankruptcies, liquidations, and reorganizations. As a result, these funds own lots of debt securities, even buying the IOUs of bankrupt companies. The funds' payoff comes when a bankrupt company regains its financial health. This style of investing is low on risk, since securities are usually bought at distress prices. Nevertheless, the returns have been high.

How such a fund performs has more to do with individual situations—*when* and *how* one company emerges from bankruptcy—than the ebb and flow of the stock market. For this reason, a fund like Mutual Shares could well complement your holdings of more traditional growth funds whose performances are more in sync with the overall market.

Not all funds that identify themselves with "value" or "growth" in their names follow the value investing strategy. And, of course, most funds have neither growth nor value in their names, so you must figure out their strategies by studying their portfolios.

Bridging the growth and value styles is the Fidelity Magellan Fund, the megafund that's perhaps the best-known mutual fund in America. Magellan is a growth fund with a broad charter. Its portfolio combines growth stocks with value stocks—anything that can deliver an above-average rate of return. With $31.7 billion in assets, the fund must invest in nearly every corner of the market. Other funds that blend growth and value are the Fidelity Retirement Growth, IAI Regional Fund, Janus, and Neuberger & Berman Manhattan funds.

Blue-chip companies, including many in the petroleum industry, are prime choices for growth-and-Income investors.

Growth-and-Income Funds

Growth funds have long been the mainstay of the equity fund lineup, but growth-and-income funds are not far behind. There are fewer growth-and-income funds than pure growth funds, but they tend to have more assets under management.

Although they're larger and therefore supposedly slower to react, growth-and-income funds have delivered returns nearly as high as the riskier growth funds. Unlike growth funds—which above all stress capital appreciation—growth-and-income funds give equal weight to capital gains and dividend income. This means they buy some of the same stocks you'll find in growth funds, such as AT&T, Federal National Mortgage Association, and General Electric. But mainly you'll find blue-chip companies paying high dividends with little growth potential, such as those found in the Dow Jones Industrial Average and the S&P 500—Exxon, Texaco, and DuPont, to name a few. At one time IBM was popular with growth-and-income fund managers, but that was before the company slashed its dividend twice.

The emphasis on blue-chips explains why these funds frequently perform so well. Their middle-of-the-road approach to investing seems to work well for Individual Retirement Accounts (IRAs) and employee-directed retirement programs.

Today, 4 of the 10 largest equity funds go for growth and income: Investment Company of America, Washington Mutual Investors, Vanguard/Windsor, and Vanguard Index 500 funds. With today's higher taxes, though, and the possibility of reduced taxes on capital gains, many investors are once again more interested in growth than dividends. Still, growth-and-income funds will continue to be a favorite.

Like growth funds, growth-and-income funds demonstrate a variety of investment styles. Many prefer value over growth stocks, since value stocks produce more dividend income. The

Burnham Fund keeps 20 percent or so of its assets in bonds, even when the stock market bulls are running rampant. Janus Growth & Income Fund promises to keep at least 25 percent of the fund in fixed-income securities and another 25 percent in growth stocks. Dean Witter Dividend Growth Securities and the Franklin Rising Dividends Fund buy the stocks with the best potential to increase dividends over the years. John Hancock Sovereign Investors won't even consider adding a stock to its portfolio unless it has a ten-year record of consistent dividend growth.

If you like the idea of investing in the entire S&P 500 instead of a few stocks of which it's comprised, you can buy an index fund such as the Vanguard Index 500 which maintains a portfolio designed to behave just like the index itself. These S&P Index funds are considered growth-and-income oriented. You may also want to look at the Gateway Index Plus fund, both an index and an options fund. Gateway's portfolio apes the performance of the S&P 100 (a smaller sampling of the 500). Because this fund sells options, and the most actively traded index options are written on the S&P 100, it makes sense to work in the most liquid market.

An option is simply a contract that gives the owner the right to buy or sell a particular stock at a set price for a limited amount of time, usually less than nine months. An option fund first invests in a portfolio of dividend-paying stocks and then "writes" (or sells) "call" options against those stocks. There is no risk because if the options are exercised, the fund already owns the stock it would have to deliver. The proceeds from the sale of these "calls" combine with the regular dividends to provide more income from the portfolio and to help protect the fund against small declines in stock prices.

In the investment world, this is considered a conservative strategy. But in selling covered calls, the mutual fund is giving up any chance of earning profits from large stock price increases during the period the option is in effect. If the market zooms, the option fund will be left behind.

This option-writing strategy usually works best when stocks move "sideways" in a narrow trading range. In such a market, few stocks rise enough to get called away, so writing "covered calls" is like pulling money out of the air or writing an insurance policy against which nobody makes a claim.

Fund managers monitor stock performance and offer advice on when to buy or sell.

Utilities (such as solar power, shown here) are good investments for equity-income funds.

Equity-Income Funds

If you think collecting dividends is the best thing about owning stocks, you'll like equity-income funds. Their mission is simple: provide shareholders with an above-average yield from a portfolio of mainly dividend-paying stocks. Equity-income funds try to deliver a higher return than the S&P 500 average, and they generally fulfill expectations with a yield at least 50 percent greater than that index. You don't have to be a stock market whiz to figure out that if a fund generates higher than normal dividends, something is going to be below normal—and that's stock price appreciation.

For instance, equity-income funds often buy utilities stocks because their dividends may grow to double those of industrial companies. But since regulators set utility rates, their growth potential is limited. Equity-income funds also invest in big oil companies such as Texaco and Royal Dutch Petroleum, again slow- or no-growth stocks with fat dividends.

Though equity-income funds are bound to trail the stock market in good times, they usually fall less when the market slides. A large dividend stream is a good defense against falling stock prices.

The big drawback for equity-income funds and, indeed, any fund that has a high payout, is higher taxes. An equity-income fund may leave you with less after-tax income than a pure growth fund, but not if owned within a tax-deferred retirement plan.

Buying stocks for their dividends seems so simple you might wonder why you need a mutual fund to do it. But to know whether a stock is really a good buy you must ask why the dividend is so high. That takes probing and analysis best left to the professionals who run this type of mutual fund.

Income Funds

Income funds are the mirror image of growth funds. Portfolio managers run these funds to produce income, while capital gains—if any—are just a by-product. Over recent years the income funds have been about half as volatile as the stock market. Their relatively high yields and stable net asset values make them attractive to risk-averse investors.

Not surprisingly, income funds want to own stocks with hearty dividends. Among major holdings of income funds are IBM, Texaco, and American Express. The difference between the stock holdings of equity-income funds and pure income funds is more in the *quantity* than the *quality* of stock they hold.

Several preferred stock funds—such as Putnam Corporate Asset and Vanguard Preferred Stock—are also considered income funds. Preferred stock funds were originally meant for corporate investors, who can take advantage of the partial tax break they get on the dividends of other corporations. But in today's yield-hungry world, these funds look good to individual taxpayers, too. Income funds devote a large portion of their assets to bonds and money-market instruments. For nearly a decade, the Wellesley Income Fund has maintained a ratio of two dollars in investment grade bonds for every dollar in equity assets.

Income funds look their best in the depths of a bear market, having lost much less of their investors' money than other fund categories, but they can gain in bull markets, too. If income funds zig while growth funds zag, they can provide welcome diversification to any portfolio.

Chapter 3

Bond Funds

Just as there are funds that specialize in buying stocks, there are other funds that specialize in buying bonds. Since a bond is fundamentally a very different investment vehicle than a share of stock, it's only natural for bond funds to operate and behave quite differently from stock funds.

When interest rates go up, bond prices go down. When rates decline, bond prices rise. Understand this see-saw relationship and you're well on your way to understanding bond, or fixed-income, mutual funds.

As you can see from table 3.1, the longer the maturity, the more sensitive the bond is to changes in interest rates. But the see-saw relationship is always there.

This relationship between interest rates and bond prices is one of the most fundamental in all of finance. It's far different from that between interest

Table 3.1

How Changes in Interest Rates Affect Bond Prices

KEY: RATES FALL 1%, PRICES RISE BY.../ RATES RISE 1%, PRICES FALL BY...

Coupon	Maturity			
▼	1 year	5 years	10 years	30 years
5%	.97%/–.96%	4.49%/–4.27%	8.18%/–7.79%	17.38%/–13.8%
6%	.96%/–.95%	4.38%/–4.16%	7.79%/–7.11%	15.45%/–12.47%
7%	.96%/–.94%	4.27%/–4.06%	7.44%/–6.8%	13.84%/–11.31%
8%	.95%/–.94%	4.16%/–3.96%	7.11%/–6.5%	12.47%/–10.32%

rates and a CD (certificate of deposit) or a money-market account, which don't fluctuate in value but instead simply pay interest.

Bond funds can fluctuate in value—even if made up entirely of U.S. government guaranteed securities or insured municipal bonds. The guarantee only assures that interest will be paid on time and that the bond will be redeemed at face value *when it matures*. Until then, its market value can and does vary. U.S. Treasury bonds are considered to have no credit risk, but their prices still vary minute to minute based entirely on changes in the interest-rate picture.

How much a bond fund fluctuates depends on the average maturity date of the portfolio, a figure often given in describing particular funds and readily available from the fund's management office. Remember, the longer the time remaining until maturity, the more sensitive bond prices are to changes in interest rates. As a rule, therefore, the net asset value of a fund comprised of long-term bonds will fluctuate more than a fund of intermediate-term bonds, and a short-term bond fund will be the least volatile of the three.

When you're only able to accept a small risk to generate a significant fixed income, choose intermediate- or long-term bond funds. If you're worried about fluctuations in net asset value, keep your money in short-term bond funds. If you're not ready for any risk, stick with money-markets.

There's an important difference between owning a bond fund and owning the bonds themselves. Most bonds pay interest twice a year, a predetermined amount on predetermined dates. A 20-year, $1,000 bond with a 7 percent interest rate will make a $35 payment every six months for the next 20 years.

Most bond funds, however, distribute income monthly, and not always the same amount, just whatever they've earned during the month. Some funds attempt to smooth out the income distributions by paying a fixed amount per share per month. Some months the fund earns more, some months less, but it knows its average income accurately enough to pay it out evenly during the year. When interest rates fall, however, the monthly payout must eventually drop to reflect the reduced income.

There's another major difference between direct ownership of bonds and owning shares in a bond fund. If you own a 10-year bond, for example, you know that next year it will be a 9-year bond; in 2 years, an 8-year; and so forth until maturity or sale. Although interest rates may go up and down in the meantime, the maturity of your bonds shortens every year, and their relative price volatility decreases accordingly. Bond funds, however, never "mature." Instead, they keep selling shorter-term bonds and buying longer-term bonds to maintain a certain maturity forever.

The basic relationship between average maturity and volatility of bond funds holds true, whether your fund is taxable or tax-free, government or corporate.

The creditworthiness of the issuer comes into play—in a small way—with corporate and municipal bonds rated AAA, AA, A, or BBB by Standard & Poor's, or Aaa, Aa, A, or Baa by Moody's Investor Services (see table 3.2). These are called "investment-grade" bonds. Anything rated lower is called "junk" or "high-yield" bonds. Credit considerations may overwhelm interest rate forces in setting prices on some of these "junk" bonds.

The highest ratings in the junk sector, sometimes called "quality junk," are BB and B. Some of the quality junk bonds are issued by companies that were formerly blue-chips but have recently taken on enormous debts in leveraged buyouts, takeovers, or other financial restructurings.

Bonds rated CCC and lower—down to D for default, which means they are no longer paying interest—include bonds of companies and government agencies in or near bankruptcy.

Since interest rates are the driving force in the bond market, the variations in returns from bond funds are not as dramatic as those from equities. Let's see how this works in practice. During a recent year, for example, the best government bond fund delivered a total return of 21.2 percent; the worst, 0.4 percent—a range of about 21 percentage points. But during the same year, the best small-company fund delivered a 46.6 percent return; the worst, 0.2 percent—more than double the variation in government bond funds.

When looking at bond funds, remember that a fund's *yield* is not the same as its *total return*, which includes yield plus or minus any change in net asset value. A fund with a 12 percent yield but only a 2 percent total return clearly lost 10 percent of its asset value during the year. In an

Table 3.2

A Guide to Bond Credit Ratings

RATING		
S&P	Moody's	
AAA	Aaa	Amoco, Exxon, and J. P. Morgan are a few of the dwindling number of borrowers in this very exclusive club.
AA	Aa	Here's where you'll find AT&T and many other phone companies. Also McDonald's, Toys'R'Us, and Wal-Mart.
A	A	Hard times sent IBM's credit rating down along with its stock price, but the credit quality is still high.
BBB	Baa	The lowest rating a bond can receive and still be considered an investment-grade security.
BB	Ba	The highest ranking for junk bonds, sometimes known as "quality junk."
B	B	Many leveraged buyouts issue bonds in this category, which suggests some doubt about the borrower's ability to repay.
CCC	Caa	Suggests an increased likelihood of default.
CC	Ca	Another rung lower on the credit ladder.
C	C	The pits. At Moody's, this means default.
D	na	Interest and/or principal payments in arrears.

up market, a bond fund's total return should exceed its yield because of the increase in bond prices. When comparing bond funds, be sure to compare yields with yields, and total returns with total returns.

Now that you're familiar with the basics of bond funds, let's look at several of the broader categories—corporate, international, government, and municipal.

The corporate group divides into high-yield, high-quality, and general-purpose funds.

Bond funds that invest abroad include both short-term, longer-term "world" bond funds.

Besides general government funds, there are also government funds that own just Treasuries, funds that invest in mortgage-backed securities, and funds that buy adjustable-rate mortgage securities (ARMs).

Municipal funds are categorized geographically. "National" funds invest in tax-exempts from across the country. Single-state bond funds provide investors from a particular state with an easy way to obtain income free of state taxes.

The Corporate Funds

High-Yield Corporate Funds

High-yield corporate bond funds have soared in recent years when interest rates fell and the stock market boomed. But anyone who owned these funds in the mid-1980s when they first became popular suffered tremendous portfolio losses in 1989 and 1990, during the "junk bond debacle."

The character of junk bond investing has shifted over the years. Until the late 1970s nearly all junk bonds were "fallen angels," bonds of once investment-grade companies that had fallen upon hard times. But then, investment banker Michael Milken of Drexel Burnham Lambert pioneered the idea of original-issue junk bonds. First, Milken used the bonds to raise money for capital-hungry emerging growth companies. One of the best known of the early junk bond issuers was MCI Communications Corporation. Later, corporate raiders and others issued junk bonds to raise funds to take over big companies or to finance leveraged buyouts (LBOs)—purchases of companies that are made with mostly borrowed funds.

In the 1990s, there have been few takeover- or LBO-related junk bonds issued. Instead, many of the newest bonds come from companies borrowing for the first time or from established borrowers refinancing debt at today's lower rates. The original premise behind junk bond investing is simple: Although riskier than high-quality bonds—and some undeniably went into default—the vast majority of junk bonds continue to pay interest. Investing in a few junk bonds is a dicey proposition, but a well-diversified portfolio of junk bonds can produce enough regular income to more than make up for losses from occasional defaults. That's why mutual funds are the natural home for such junk bond portfolios.

What's more, today's junk bond issuers are better positioned to repay their debts. They have income of about \$2.30 for every \$1 in interest owed; at the height of the junk-bond fling, in 1988, the comparable figure was only \$1.30.

All this suggests that some fixed-income investors might want to give junk bonds another look. Equity investors might consider junk funds, too, because of their "equity-like returns"—that is, returns that are closer to those from stocks than from bonds.

Junk bond funds display many investment styles. As a result, their

portfolios—and their returns—are far more varied than, say, government or municipal bond funds. Most have the lion's share of their assets in B-rated bonds. Some, like Phoenix High-Yield, have gone global in their search for high-yield instruments, cashing in on a recent boom in bonds from emerging markets. The more conservative funds, like Nicholas and Vanguard Fixed-Income High-Yield Corporate Portfolio, buy higher-rated bonds, including U.S. Treasury bonds.

One of the more unusual high-yield funds is Fidelity Capital & Income, keeping about half its portfolio in bonds that are in default, distress, and bankruptcy. It also takes an active role in corporate restructurings, even joining creditors' committees in bankruptcy proceedings. In early 1994, the portfolio manager of Fidelity Capital & Income Fund emerged as one of the major creditors and key players in the battle over the bankrupt department store chain, R. H. Macy & Company.

High-Quality Corporate Funds

If you examine the portfolios of all the high-quality corporate bond funds, you might think you have the wrong label on them. Of their 25 largest holdings, 18 are U.S. Treasury notes or bonds. Seven holdings are mortgage-backed securities guaranteed by the U.S. government, and only one is a corporate issue.

There's no question these securities provide high credit quality (see table 3.3). But shouldn't a corporate bond fund hold mainly corporate bonds? Perhaps. But sometimes it takes a liberal helping of Treasury bonds to maintain the overall credit quality of these funds. For the last several years, high-quality corporate debt has become scarce, while U.S. Treasury securities—issued to finance ballooning budget deficits—have become far more plentiful. If the rates paid by government and high-quality corporate bonds become close enough, then the government bonds with their lower risk may be the better investment for these funds. Of course, if the economy is nearing or is currently in a recession, government securities are the bonds of choice.

Few new high-quality corporate bond funds opened for business during the 1980s, and existing funds did not grow as fast as other funds during the period. For investors who prized safety, government bond funds produced fine returns. For those who reached out for yield, junk bond funds were far more alluring. Other factors worked against investment-grade corporates in favor of government bonds—and still do. First, there's the chance of a financially sound company suffering business reversals and thus losing its top-drawer rating. That's what happened to IBM.

Table 3.3

High-Quality Corporate Funds

BEST RETURNS

Period	Fund	Total Return*
1993	Dreyfus A Bonds Plus	15.0%
1991–93	Vanguard F/I L/T Corp.	15.0
1989–93	Vanguard F/I L/T Corp.	13.2

*Average annual, pretax

The ailing computer giant is still solid but no longer on top of the heap.

There are also other concerns. In October 1988, when the management of RJR Nabisco first raised the possibility of a leveraged buyout, which would vastly increase the debt load and destroy the company's investment-grade rating, the company's bonds plunged 15 percent in price. The risk that bonds will tumble in price because of a takeover—or even a *threatened* takeover—is called "event risk." In recent years some corporations have issued bonds that attempt to safeguard the rights of bondholders, but the vast majority of corporate bonds don't have such protections.

Finally, there's "call risk." Most corporate bonds, junk bonds included, give the issuer the right to redeem the bonds, or "call" them, well before maturity. If interest rates drop, issuers try to call their bonds and refinance the debt at a lower rate. (This is basically the same idea as refinancing your home mortgage to take advantage of lower interest rates.) Calls are bad news for bondholders. True, the bondholders collect a premium for their bonds: The issuer may pay $1,030 or $1,050 for a $1,000 bond. But that's small consolation to bondholders who must reinvest the proceeds at the current, lower interest rate.

A mutual fund with a large number of callable bonds might find itself in just such a quandary. Part of a bond fund manager's job is to steer around such obstacles, either by buying bonds whose original rates are so low they're unlikely to be called or by purchasing government bonds, which can't be called.

In recent years, some investment-grade bond funds that concentrated on short-term securities did a land-rush business. For the most part, though, high-quality bond funds perform about as well as government funds. That's no surprise, since these funds are full of government securities. If you're an investor who's picky about what bonds your mutual funds hold, you might as well invest directly in government funds.

General-Bond Corporate Funds

General-bond funds might be a happy compromise for an investor torn between two highs: high-yield and high-quality. But the category is more of a catchall than a good description of the character of the bonds in these funds' portfolios.

The more cautious funds—like Bartlett Capital Fixed-Income Fund, FPA New Income Fund, and Harbor Bond Fund—hold high-quality portfolios, solidly based in government bonds. Fidelity Short-Term Bond Fund has a big chunk of its assets in non–U.S. bonds. Alliance Bond Corporate Bond Portfolio, recently the top performer in this category (see table 3.4), made big bets

Table 3.4

Corporate General Funds

BEST RETURNS

Period	Fund	Total Return*
1993	Alliance Bond Corp. Bond	31.1%
1991–93	Fortress Bond	24.9
1989–93	Alliance Bond Corp. Bond	15.9

*Average annual, pretax

on longer maturities and lesser-rated companies, and both paid off in spades.

Somewhere in the middle are the funds with a good chunk of bonds rated A or BBB by Standard & Poor's or A and Baa by Moody's (the lowest ratings still considered investment-grade). Such bonds pay more interest than government AA-rated issues. Funds with this approach include American Capital Corporate Bond and Merrill Lynch Corporate Bond Intermediate-Term Portfolio.

Because the general-bond category is a catchall, investors must do a little homework before plunging in—including reading prospectuses. Some funds, for instance, reserve at least 65 percent of their portfolios for investment-grade securities; the only difference between these and funds in the high-quality corporate category may be what they do with the other 35 percent.

Some general corporate bond funds are "flexible" funds, with the freedom to choose the best bonds in any market conditions. One such fund, Strong Income Fund, can choose from U.S. government-backed securities to CC-rated junk bonds to foreign governments' debt, and can also use futures and options when appropriate. For a long time, this fund held only junk bonds, but after getting creamed in the junk bond massacre it switched to investment-grade bonds. In recent years, most of its portfolio was in longer-term, medium-grade bonds.

Investing in these "flexible" funds is not only for the Mississippi gambler-type investor. With the help of a knowledgeable portfolio manager these funds can meet the needs of the prudent investor, and allow for greater flexibility within the market.

These "flexible" funds usually seek whatever maturity and ratings offer the best bond investment opportunities—from government bonds to junk. Of course, if the portfolio manager misjudges the market, returns can be sub-par.

The International Funds

World Bond and Short-Term World Income Funds

A decade ago it was easy to choose the best international bond fund. MFS Worldwide Governments Trust (then known as Massachusetts Financial International Trust-Bond Portfolio) was the only international bond fund. Even in the late 1980s, there were just a handful of such funds. Now there are dozens, most of which have an average maturity of about one year. These funds attempt to earn a yield higher than money-market funds and use hedging techniques to minimize risk to investors' principal.

The bond funds, as opposed to the *international* bond funds, maintain a longer maturity—on average about six years—and rarely hedge their portfolios. They're called "world" (not "foreign") because they generally put about one-third of their portfolios into U.S. bonds.

What made foreign fixed-income securities so alluring in recent years was higher interest rates abroad than at home. Higher rates alone make the yields attractive, coupled with the generally declining dollar, which enhanced total returns even more. For example, if your fund is earning 9 percent on German bonds and the mark appreciates 9 percent against the dollar, your total return is 18 percent. That's not bad for a bond fund, especially one with impeccable credit quality.

But what if the dollar appreciates instead of declining? In one such case, U.S. investors in world bond funds earned, on average, total returns of only 2.8 percent! PaineWebber Global Income Fund, the largest world bond fund, earned nearly 7 percent

Table 3.5

International Funds

BEST RETURNS

Period	Fund	Total Return*
World Bond		
1993	G. T. Global High-Income A	51.6%
1991–93	Scudder International Bond	15.1
1989–93	Scudder International Bond	14.6
Short-Term World Income		
1993	Fidelity S-T World Income	12.4%
1991–93	Eaton Vance S-T Global Income	6.5
1989–93	Not Available	

*Average annual, pretax

interest but produced a total return of only 1.3 percent.

The world bond fund with the highest return during that period was G. T. Global High-Income A, up 51.6 percent. It didn't earn that much by investing in Germany and France (see table 3.5). Instead, it bought "emerging markets debt"—bonds issued in Mexico, Morocco, Poland, and Argentina. Fund managers studied such factors as inflation, unemployment, and government fiscal and monetary policy before buying bonds in countries that were clearly on the road to economic reform.

The profits for successful emerging market debt funds come not only from higher interest rates but also from price appreciation of the bonds themselves, as other investors recognize the improved credit quality and bid the bonds up. Currency changes play a part in these funds, too, since many emerging nations peg their currencies to the U.S. dollar or issue dollar-denominated debt, eliminating currency fluctuations.

Of course, the risks of currency fluctuations are well known, and many funds hedge these risks with options or futures contracts. Since hedging, however, can be costly and can wipe out the extra interest paid by foreign bonds, these funds sometimes use other techniques which reduce but don't totally eliminate currency risk. One method is "dollar-hedging": keeping part of the portfolio in dollar bonds, dollar-denominated foreign-issued bonds, or bonds of currencies that more or less move in tandem with the dollar—such as the Canadian and Australian dollars. Another method is "cross-hedging": buying strong currencies, like the German mark and Swiss franc, and selling weaker ones, like the Italian lira and British pound. With such a position, a fund can earn the higher yields of the weaker currency without the risk. The cross-hedge only works, however, when the currencies stay within a fairly predictable range.

When that predictability breaks down, as it did a few years ago, Pilgrim Short-Term Multi-Market Income Fund lost more than 10 percent in one month, and dropped 15.1 percent in a year. That doesn't sound like a disaster unless you consider that many of these funds were marketed to investors as alternatives to CDs and money-market funds.

The international bond funds can provide decent returns as well as valuable diversification, especially in periods when other funds sag. Nevertheless, it's important to remember that these funds are a complement to, not a substitute for, domestic bond funds.

The Government Funds

Treasury Notes and Bonds

Funds that only invest in U.S. Treasury notes and bonds appeal to an investors' sense of security or, perhaps,

*in*security. There's no credit risk in these funds.

But there are still differences between funds. Interest-rate risk can be substantial if the fund buys bonds that don't mature until sometime into the next century (see table 3.6).

If you like money-market mutual funds, you may consider some of the shorter-term Treasury portfolios, such as Dreyfus Short-Intermediate Government Fund or Vanguard Fixed-Income Short-Term Federal Fund. The average maturity of these portfolios is three years or less, and, depending on conditions in the fixed-income markets, there could be half a percentage point or more of extra yield.

With short maturity bonds, the fund's NAV will fluctuate somewhat. Such a fund will almost always have a positive total return—which includes, you remember, interest rate payments plus or minus the change in the bonds' net asset value. Compared to longer-term funds, short-term funds look best when interest rates are rising, and worst when rates decline. But when interest rates are declining or already low, many investors have discovered them to be a good substitute for money-market mutual funds.

In longer-term funds, good portfolio managers can use a few tricks to add value and earn their fees. If a drop in interest rates is forecast, they can move fund assets into longer-term bonds, thus keeping yield relatively high during the approaching low-interest days. If it looks like interest rates are heading higher, the portfolio managers can move assets into bonds with shorter maturity dates. Although they can't avoid declining bond prices altogether, this strategy does lessen the damage.

The most extreme—and volatile—sort of long-term government securities funds are those of the Benham Target Maturities series, which invest in zero-coupon bonds. These bonds sell at a fraction of their par value, normally $1,000, and can be redeemed for their full face value when they mature. But there are no interest payments in the interim. The "interest" from a zero-coupon bond is received when you sell the bond—it's the difference between the purchase price and the face value.

Table 3.6

Government Treasury Funds

BEST RETURNS

Period	Fund	Total Return*
1993	Stagecoach U.S. Govt. Allocation	17.4%
1991–93	Benham Target Maturities 2000	14.5
1989–93	Benham Target Maturities 2000	13.8

*Average annual, pretax

Zeros make the most sense when held in a tax-deferred account. Although they pay no cash interest, the Internal Revenue Service says the zero earnings "accrete" interest every year, so you owe taxes on the interest even though you don't collect it. Some people like these bonds for children's accounts, and buy those that mature when the child reaches college age. If a child is paying tax at his or her parent's rate—and many now do—the zeros may be expensive for him or her, too.

There's no category of bond more sensitive to changes in interest rates than zero-coupon bonds. In periods of falling interest rates, the zero-coupon funds will invariably be the best performers, and the worst when interest rates rise. As short-term trading vehicles, these funds make some sense, but as long-term investments, zero-coupon bonds owned directly are the way to go. Here's why: Suppose you'll be age 65 in the year 2015. You decide to put your Individual Retirement Account funds into zero-coupon bonds which mature that year, a reasonable thing to do. Once you pay the broker's commission, you won't pay another nickel until your bonds mature. But if you buy an equivalent zero-coupon mutual fund, you'll be hit for a small percentage in expenses each and every year.

In choosing a government bond fund, watch out for funds with abnormally high yields. If the interest rate on the bellwether 30-year U.S. Treasury—often quoted on the financial pages and in broadcast business reports—is near 8 percent, be suspicious about funds that pay 9 or 10 percent. They may be loading up their portfolios with "premium" bonds, which carry higher interest rates than currently issued securities. For instance, 11.25 percent Treasury bonds that mature in February 2015 were worth $1,562.50 per bond at one point, and paid $112.50 per year in interest, $50 more than a bond reflecting the then current interest rate. Some fund managers "enhanced" their yield with such bonds.

But when these higher coupon bonds mature, they will be worth only $1,000. Under accounting rules, that premium—the price of the bond in excess over $1,000—must be "amortized" (written off) over the remaining life of the bond. Thus, for every one of these bonds, the portfolio managers must deduct about $27 a year from the value of the fund. Though premium bonds can bolster current income, they also erode the fund's principal. On the other hand, when interest rates rise, high-coupon bonds hold their values better than low-coupon bonds that sell at a discount.

To determine if a fund is juicing its yield with premium bonds, request a copy of the portfolio. If the portfolio is full of bonds paying two, three, or more interest points higher than current Treasury bond yields, there may be a "premium" investment strategy. But not always: Some funds bought these bonds when rates were far higher and have simply held on to them. In this case, the bond fund does not have to amortize the premium, but you must still think in those terms. If you buy into such a fund, you may be paying $1,400 for bonds that will eventually be worth only $1,000.

General Funds

Mutual fund marketers love to invoke Uncle Sam's goodwill in naming funds. And for good reason. Everybody trusts the U.S. government to pay its interest and principal. And the returns haven't been bad, either (see table 3.7). Some government funds lean on Treasuries, others emphasize mortgage-backed securities.

However, don't assume these funds are merely generic or can be easily substituted for one another. For starters, some funds say their objective is preservation of capital and current income, or current income consistent with preservation of capital. Others funds go for current income alone. These funds can maximize current income by taking steps that put a part of your investment in them at risk.

The EV Traditional Government Obligations Fund, for example, invests in extremes like Ginnie Maes—with either very high or very low interest rates—because they offer values that current coupon bonds don't. Deep discount securities give the portfolio upside potential in bond market rallies, while the high-premium issues cushion the fund during market slumps. The combination of extremes keeps the fund on a fairly even keel, with a 10.2 percent average annual return over a 5-year period, above average for comparable funds.

Be careful with funds that promise higher income through the use of futures and options, often known as "government plus" funds. The problem is that many of these plusses have returned minus income in recent years. Unfortunately, not all of these funds have "plus" in their names, so look closely at any government bond fund before you invest.

The plus funds looked smart back in the mid-1980s when interest rates started to fall. Yield-conscious investors, anxious to hold on to double-digit rates, saw the promises of 12 percent yields when the going rate was below 10 percent. In most cases, the plus funds bought Treasury bonds at par and sold or "wrote" call options against them. (A call option, as discussed earlier, gives the buyer the right to buy the bond at a predetermined price until a certain date. The option seller collects and keeps a fee or "premium" for writing the option.) The fund thus kept both the interest from the bonds and the premium from the options.

When interest rates remain fairly stable, the strategy pays off, but when interest rates fall and bond prices rise, plus funds lose out on some of that increase in value. Here's why: Suppose the fund bought a bond at 100 or $1,000—par value—and wrote an option to sell the bond at 102. In a rally, the bond goes to 105, and the owner of the option "exercises" it, paying only 102. The plus fund has lost three points in capital gains.

There's another potential downside to this option strategy. Suppose the fund has bonds trading at 90 that were originally purchased at par. The portfolio manager, needing to produce extra income, sells options that are exercisable at 95. If the bond market rallies and the bonds are called away at 95, the sale of the options has effectively locked in a capital loss for the fund. Where's the "plus" in that?!

The biggest problem with these plus funds showed up in 1987, when long-term interest rates rose from 7.5 percent in the spring to more than 10 percent in the fall. In such a situation, a plain vanilla government bond fund

Table 3.7

Government General Funds

BEST RETURNS

Period	Fund	Total Return*
1993	Comstock Partners Strategy O	20.5%
1991–93	Advantage Government Securities	14.3
1989–93	Advantage Government Securities	12.6

*Average annual, pretax

can minimize the damage by selling long maturity bonds and replacing them with short, less volatile maturities. Plus funds, in contrast, generally hold the longest maturity bonds because they fetch the highest option premiums, but they're also the most vulnerable to falling bond markets. True, the option-writing strategy mitigates *some* of the damage from rising rates, but only a portion.

In the end, investing in government securities is a simple business. Credit quality is not an issue: You buy for income and capital preservation. So you need a very good reason to invest in a fund that adds complications.

The Municipal Funds

National, Single-State, California, and New York Funds

No one likes higher taxes. No one, that is, except the people who sell and manage municipal bond funds. When Bill Clinton was elected president the "muni" market cheered and has been cheering ever since. His tax hikes for upper-income taxpayers make the muni alternative look better than ever. The income from muni bond funds can't be touched by the Internal Revenue Service as long as the interest income derives from tax-exempt securities issued by state and local governments and their authorities.

A tax-exempt security typically sports a lower yield and a lower total return than a taxable security of comparable maturity and credit quality, although at times muni funds can outperform taxable funds (see table 3.8). Investors will accept these lower returns to get the tax exemption. In deciding whether to invest in a muni or a taxable bond fund, the key question to ask is, "What is my taxable-equivalent to the yield from the muni fund?" The answer depends on your marginal tax rate: The higher this rate, the better a muni looks compared to a taxable fund.

To determine if muni funds are right for you, compare muni and taxable funds, adjusting for the tax exemption. For instance, in early 1994, the Vanguard Fixed-Income Long-Term U.S. Treasury Fund was yielding 6.2 percent, while the Vanguard Municipal Bond Long-Term Fund was yielding 5 percent. What's the better buy? Suppose you're in the 31 percent marginal tax bracket. You merely subtract 31 percent representing taxes on the taxable 6.2 percent yield and you see that you would get to keep only 4.3 percent. Obviously, the muni fund offers a better after-tax yield.

There's another way to calculate this. Start with the number 1 and subtract your marginal tax bracket from it: 1 minus 0.31 (31 percent is also expressed as 0.31) equals 0.69. Next, you divide that number into the tax-exempt yield. Divide 5 percent by 0.69 and you get 7.3 percent. This shows that, unless you can get a return of at least 7.3 percent in a taxable investment of like quality, the muni is the better deal.

Muni bond income is free from federal taxes but your state may tax muni income from bonds issued by other states. Neither the New Yorker

Table 3.8

Government Mortgage Funds

BEST RETURNS

Period	Fund	Total Return*
1993	Alliance Mortg. Secs. Income B	9.4%
1991–93	Princor Government Secs. Income	10.6
1989–93	Vanguard Fixed-Income GNMA	10.8

*Average annual, pretax

Table 3.9

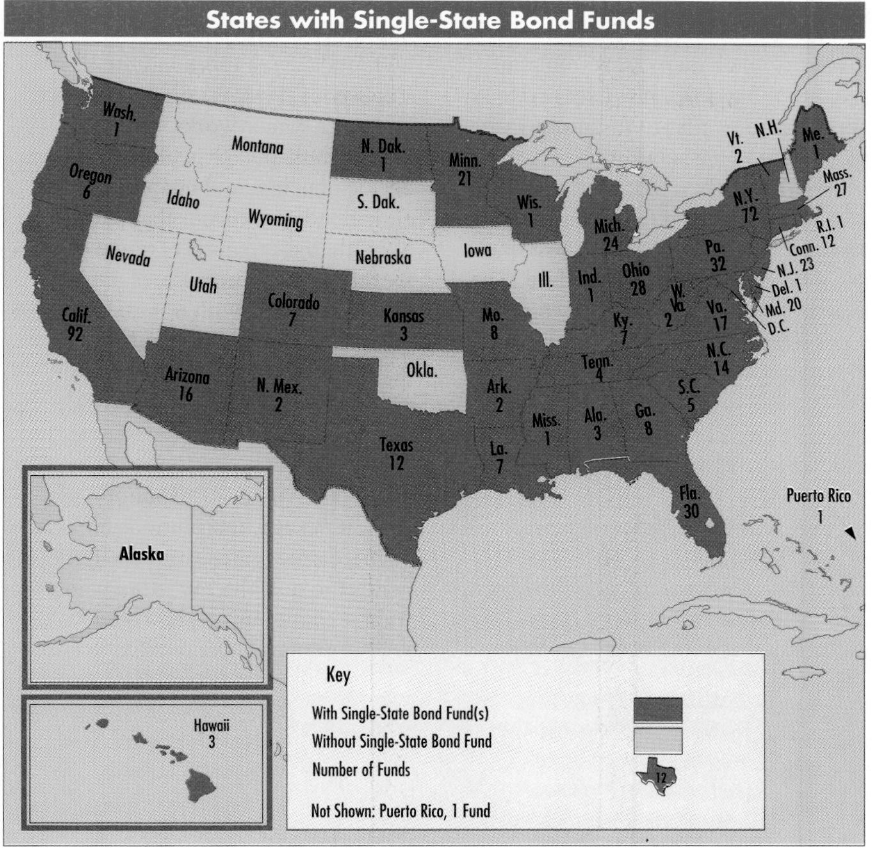

investing in a California bond nor the Californian with the New York bond will owe federal tax on the interest, but he or she will owe state income tax. In states with low-income tax rates, that may not matter. But in high tax states like California and New York, the extra tax can cut into your returns. So the mutual fund folks have come up with an antidote for that, too: single-state municipal bond funds. By restricting investment to the investor's home state, these funds generate income exempt not only from federal taxes but also from state and city income taxes.

For the tax-weary folks of New York City, a New York bond fund is said to be "triple-tax-exempt." The largest municipal fund of all, in fact, is the Franklin California Tax-Free Income Fund. It's also one of the oldest, dating back to 1977.

You don't have to live in a big, heavily populated state to have a single-state fund to call your own. These funds now cover 38 states and Puerto Rico (see table 3.9). If a state isn't represented, the tax laws may not be amenable to it, and if there's no state income or personal property assessment that taxes financial holdings, there's no need for a single-state muni fund—though Texas has 12 of them anyway. Illinois, for instance, does have a state income tax but does not exempt interest earned from most Illinois municipal bonds. So there's no particular advantage for an Illinois taxpayer to invest in most Illinois bonds.

The big drawback of single-state funds is apparent in the name itself: All the bonds come from a single state and rise and fall on the financial condition of the state, its local governments, and its bond-issuing authorities.

Insured funds are popular with investors since many governments seem to move from one fiscal crisis to another. Ironically, high-quality bonds of well-known issuers aren't always a safe harbor. When the muni market gets the shakes, the first bonds to get dumped are those of the highest quality, since they're the most liquid. The lesser credits and lesser-known names seem to hold up relatively well, provided they don't default. Many muni funds achieve "high yield" by seeking out the higher interest rates of the little-known issuers.

If you've decided to invest in tax-exempt funds, you face the same kinds of decisions you make with taxable funds. Do you want a fund with short-, intermediate-, or long-term bonds? Is there a single-state fund for your home state, and is the yield competitive? Finally, do you want investment-grade, insured, or junk municipal bonds?

The menu of muni offerings is broad, so a good fund can diversify its portfolio both geographically and by the type of project the bonds finance.

General obligation (GO) bonds—those backed by the credit and taxing power of the issuer—are only a small part of the muni bond lineup. Far more numerous are revenue bonds, paid off by rentals, fees, tolls, and the like from roads, bridges, tunnels, arenas, ballparks, water works, sewage treatment plants, power plants, parking decks, housing, and hospitals. Revenue bonds are riskier than GOs—after all, the project's revenue can easily fall short of projections, a not uncommon risk with nonessential public projects like arenas and stadiums. A project can also run far over budget or never be completed.

If your fund manager has racked up capital gains, the fund will have to make this type of distribution, too. Although such distributions are infrequent, capital gains from tax-free bonds are taxable. Investors who don't want capital gains should stick to yield-oriented funds that emphasize bonds selling above par. Such funds don't climb as much in a falling rate environment, nor do they melt as quickly if interest rates climb.

Like their taxable counterparts, muni funds are creatures of interest rates. But munis don't move in lockstep with Treasuries, and at times they can be more volatile.

Chapter 4

Money-Market Funds

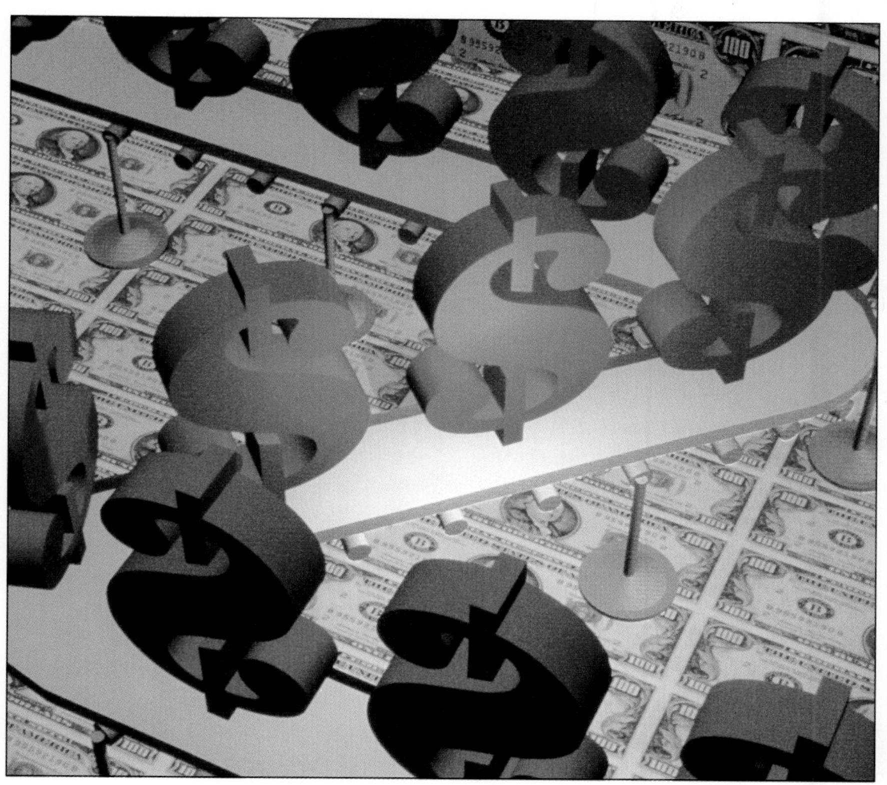

A third type of mutual fund invests in bondlike instruments for their current interest rather than any type of appreciation. These funds aim to pay daily interest and retain instant liquidity, just like a savings account at a local bank. But because they invest and earn interest, the tax treatment of their earnings can—and does—vary. Here's the breakdown.

Taxable Money-Market Funds

Money-market funds are extremely popular with investors. They are the safest mutual fund investments around, even rivaling the security of a bank account. In fact, both types of funds are similar in some ways: interest earned is usually credited daily, and the payments to investors, while technically "dividends," are the functional equivalent of interest.

Unlike stocks and bonds, money-market funds buy and sell very short-term securities from the highest-rated corporations—including many overnight transactions. As a result, they are able to maintain their net asset value constant at $1 per share. The small profits and losses in the portfolio can be accounted for by varying the payout. If there's a capital gain, the fund just passes it along as extra yield, while small losses can be covered by daily income. Many funds use an accounting method that allows them to carry the securities on their books at cost. Under those rules, assets don't fluctuate in value at all.

Since money-market funds share so many commonalities with bank accounts, it's not surprising that many people use them that way. Their yields have been higher—on average about one percentage point more—than bank money-market accounts. That's because money-market funds pass along to their investors all they earn—minus expenses, of course. A bank money-market fund is an administered rate. The bank decides what it will pay on money-market deposits and tends to pay only what it must to keep deposits. When loan demand is weak, many banks will lower their interest rates to encourage depositors to withdraw their money.

Like bank accounts, most money-market funds offer some kind of check-writing privileges. However, they usually require a minimum check amount of several hundred dollars, and may also impose other restrictions.

Despite the restrictions, you might find it convenient to maintain a money-market fund along with your other Franklin, Putnam, or Scudder mutual funds. This allows you to move money into and out of your other funds more conveniently, with the money-market fund serving as a good parking place for money you don't want in one of the other funds. With a money-market fund, your assets earn interest daily.

Since there's a great deal of similarity in money-market investment policies and services, investors shopping for stock or bond funds generally pay little attention to the fund family's associated money-market funds. Compared to the risks of a growth fund versus a balanced fund, the difference between money funds is trivial.

But there *are* tiny differences. If you look at money-market fund yields in a newspaper's financial section, you'll see as much as two percentage points of difference between funds. That, however, can be deceptive. In the very short term, yields are volatile, and any week's yield will depend on the various maturities of each fund. The shorter the maturity, the faster the yield will respond to changes in interest rates. Suppose one fund has an average maturity of 30 days and another averages 15 days. When interest rates rise, the yield on the 15-day fund goes up faster, because the fund has more investments to roll over at higher interest rates. But if interest rates fall, the longer maturity fund fares better

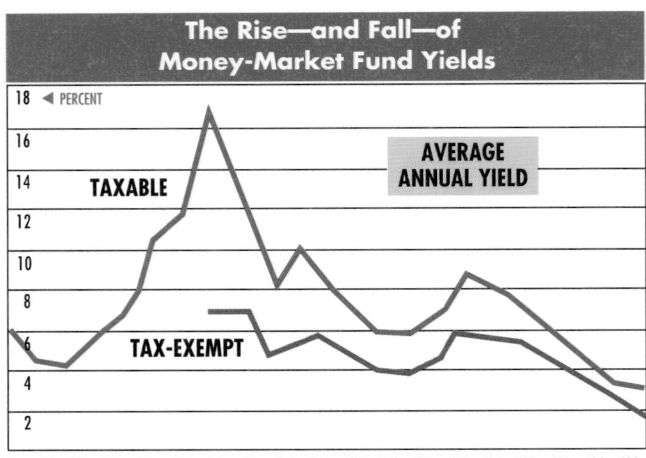

Money-Market funds are popular with investors because they are considered the safest mutual funds investment.

because it has more time remaining on its higher-yielding investments.

Over a one-year period, however, these differences smooth out. In fact, *Income & Safety,* a newsletter that tracks money-market funds, says that the difference between the highest- and lowest-yielding fund in any year is about 0.9 percentage points—only $90 less income per year on a $10,000 average balance. Of course, the larger the average balance in your money-market fund, the more significant this becomes.

One reason for this homogeneity is that money-market funds must live within fairly narrow strictures set down by industry practice and the Securities & Exchange Commission (SEC). Funds mainly invest in U.S. Treasury bills, repurchase agreements, bank certificates of deposit, banker's acceptances, and commercial paper. Following is a brief description of each:

U.S. Treasury bills. These are short-term obligations of the U.S. government, which come in three-month, six-month, and one-year maturities. Individual investors can buy these on their own, with a $10,000 minimum. The securities of other U.S. government agencies—including the Farm Credit Bank, Federal National Mortgage Association, Federal Home Loan Mortgage Corporation, and the Student Loan Marketing Association—are also permissible for many funds.

Repurchase agreements. "Repo's," as they're commonly known, are short-term borrowings using U.S. government securities as collateral. A bank or securities dealer with an inventory of Treasury bonds borrows cash from a money-market fund and gives the fund the securities as collateral for the loan, which lasts anywhere from overnight to, say, 20 days. This arrangement is called a repurchase agreement because the borrower agrees to "repurchase" the collateral by paying back the loan. As long as the fund can keep the securities in case of default, the credit quality is considered high.

Bank certificates of deposit. Most people are familiar with CDs. Money-market funds invest in "jumbo" CDs, with face amounts over $100,000 and no FDIC insurance. The creditworthiness of the issuing bank is the only security. Sometimes money-market funds invest in Eurodollar CDs, which are dollar-based CDs issued by European (usually London) branches of U.S. banks, with interest rates a little higher than those of domestic CDs. Yankee CDs are issued in the United States by branches of foreign banks.

Banker's acceptances. These are irrevocable obligations of the banks that issue them, so their quality is similar to that of a bank's certificate of deposit. Acceptances are created as a financing tool for international trade, but holders of the acceptances can raise cash immediately by selling them into the money market. Money-market funds often buy banker's acceptances.

Commercial paper. As a less-costly alternative to bank borrowings, many large corporations raise funds through short-term IOUs called "commercial paper." The only backing is the credit-worthiness of the issuer.

If you look behind the yields available on these instruments, you see why all money fund yields lie within a narrow range. When T-bills yield 3 percent, high-grade commercial paper yields 3.2 percent, and CDs about 2.8 percent. In such an interest-rate environment, there's little value a portfolio manager can add by actively trading assets, and there's no way a money fund could earn 4 percent. Naturally, when T-bills and other government securities pay higher interest rates, other rates follow.

The major difference between the performance of one money fund as compared to another depends on overhead. All money funds are sold without sales fees, but there can be hidden charges, called "12(b-1)" fees, when you sell. Choose a fund with expenses—management fees and other costs such as printing, mailing, and auditing—totaling less than 0.50 percent. When yields are low, expenses are that much more important. Remember, expenses of 0.50 percent on a 3 percent yield remove one-sixth of your income.

While credit quality has emerged as a major concern in the last few years, historically money-market funds have been a good way to go. In the nearly twenty-year history of money-market funds, no fund investor has lost any principal, but some are worried because there has never been so much debt outstanding in the U.S. economy.

To ward off potential problems in the money funds, the Securities & Exchange Commission has pulled in its reins in recent years. First, it lowered the ceiling on the maximum average maturity of a money-market fund portfolio from 120 days to 90 days. In general, the closer the maturity date of a security or portfolio, the lower the risk of owning it. Second, the SEC prohibited funds from investing in below-investment-grade commercial paper. Third, no more than 5 percent of a fund can be invested in the lowest tier of investment-grade paper, rated A-2 by Standard & Poor's and P-2 by Moody's. This rule came on the heels of two defaults by issuers of junk commercial paper held in part by two money-market funds. In both cases, fund shareholders were spared losses because the funds' managers, Value Line Inc., and T. Rowe Price Associates, made up the losses. But they were under no legal obligation to make their investors whole.

Finally, the SEC made exotic fixed-income investments such as "inverse floaters" off limits to money-market funds. Such instruments have gained a following among a handful of money fund managers. As interest rates came down, the interest payments paid by these vehicles actually went up. But if interest rates went up, the interest payments—along with the principal value—went down. This threatened to undermine the money funds' ability to maintain a $1 net asset value, so regulators scotched it.

Many investors are intrigued by the obvious benefits of short-term state tax-exempt funds.

(Inverse floaters can still be used in funds with fluctuating NAVs.)

Investors can avoid credit quality questions by sticking to U.S. government money-market funds, which buy securities free of credit risk but pay lower yields. In times of economic uncertainty, many fund analysts advise selecting the government funds, particularly if you don't have to settle for a lesser return. By careful fund shopping it's possible to find some government funds with better yields than those which also include bank CDs and commercial paper, and if you switch from a general-purpose to a government money-market fund in the same fund family, the difference in yields may be no more than 0.20 or 0.30 percentage points—a small price to pay to lessen the worry about credit quality.

U.S. government funds also have another virtue that's sometimes overlooked. Just as the federal government doesn't tax interest earned by investing in state and local government debt, most state and local governments don't tax interest earned on federal government debt. If you are in a high-tax state like New York or California, such a tax exemption can add as much as one percentage point to a fund's effective yield.

Not all government funds qualify for this tax treatment. Interest from repurchase agreements doesn't count, because the income is coming not from the government securities but from the borrower posting the securities as collateral for a loan. By the same token, many general-purpose funds invest in Treasury securities anyhow, and the portion of income generated by these securities should be exempt from state and local taxes.

Tax-Exempt Money-Market Funds

Tax-exempt money-market funds have many of the same characteristics and features as taxable money funds: short-maturity securities, liquidity, and check-writing privileges. But what makes these different—and so alluring to many investors—is that the income is beyond the Internal Revenue Service's reach.

These funds escape taxes by investing in short-term instruments issued by state, county, and municipal governments and public authorities. For instance, most communities collect taxes several times a year, but their need for cash doesn't totally conform to that same tax collection schedule. So they issue tax anticipation notes, short-term borrowings meant to provide cash for the municipality or agency until tax receipts roll in. In similar fashion, bond anticipation notes are issued as temporary financing until long-term bonds can be sold, as well as revenue anticipation notes, which help keep a government unit in operation until other revenue (such as a federal grant) is received.

Tax-free money funds also rely heavily on "put bonds" and variable-rate demand notes. In these securities, the interest rate is reset frequently, sometimes as often as every seven days. If the fund manager doesn't like the new interest rate, he or she can always "put"—or give back—the bonds to the issuer for redemption. But this is rare. Rates are generally set to be competitive with other current rates in the tax-exempt market.

Such bonds, often backed with a bank letter of credit to assure investors the money to redeem them will be there, almost always trade at par. That makes them especially good investments for money-market type funds that strive to hold their net asset values constant. In fact, investment bankers devised these floating-rate securities largely to meet the needs of tax-exempt money-market funds.

When considering tax-free funds, remember the income may be taxable by state and local government. States usually exempt income from municipal securities issued in their state, but they don't care about those issued elsewhere. Thus, a general purpose tax-exempt money-market fund may not be totally tax free. If you're a Michigan resident, for example, and only 5 percent of the income generated by your tax-free fund came from Michigan securities, the Michigan tax folks will still take their bite out of the remaining 95 percent of your supposed tax-free income.

For many investors, this may not be much of a bother. If the local tax is minimal, the tax-free fund may remain a great deal. But if you live in California, Connecticut, Massachusetts, Michigan, Missouri, New Jersey, New York, Ohio, or Pennsylvania, you need not pay any taxes on your tax-free money-market fund income. You can find funds that invest solely in short-term securities of governments and public authorities from any one of those states. All the income passes to you untaxed.

The most important consideration when looking at tax-free money funds is your marginal tax bracket—including federal, state, and local tax rates. The bigger the bite from all these, the better a tax-free fund is going to feel. A New York City resident paying the top marginal tax rate will find the yield on a "triple-tax-exempt" money-market fund very attractive ("triple" means it's free from federal, state, and city income taxes).

Single-state tax-free funds suffer some drawbacks, however. For example, the portfolios lack geographical diversification. If the state in which you reside undergoes fiscal woes, that will hurt all municipal securities issued in that state. If the state can fix its problems, such troubles will be temporary.

Another potential problem is a shortage of investments. If money pours into the fund faster than it can find creditworthy investments, it may have to buy some out-of-state securities. This happened to the Massachusetts Tax-Free Fund and also the Spartan New Jersey Tax-Free Fund. In such cases, a portion of the funds' earnings will wind up subject to state income tax.

Chapter 5

Other Types of Mutual Funds

Now that you know something of the pure and simple equity and bond funds, and the money markets, let's look briefly at other—less "pure"—types of mutual funds.

Balanced Funds

Balanced funds are the "sensible shoes" of the mutual fund business—prudent, practical, and, yes, boring. With these funds you get stocks for growth and bonds for income—and a portfolio manager to worry about how much of each you need. There's nothing trendy about balanced funds, either. They are among the oldest of all mutual funds. Vanguard/Wellington Fund opened shop in 1928, the CGM Mutual Fund (formerly known as Loomis-Sayles Mutual) in 1929, and about a dozen more date to the 1930s. CGM Mutual, incidentally, is one of the best-balanced funds over the intermediate and long term (see table 5.1).

Balanced funds are based on the principle that stock and bond prices go

Table 5.1

Balanced Funds

BEST RETURNS

Period	Fund	Total Return*
1993	CGM Mutual	21.8%
1991–93	Evergreen Foundation	23.7
1989–93	CGM Mutual	17.5
1984–93	CGM Mutual	16.7

*Average annual, pretax

in opposite directions. In a booming economy, stocks rise because of improving corporate profitability. The boom also creates increased demand for credit, so interest rates rise and bond prices fall. In a recession, however, the opposite happens: stocks fall and bonds rise. Of course, there are occasionally times when stocks and bonds rise or fall together.

These funds' long histories may give comfort to some investors and steer them around trouble spots. For instance, balanced funds commonly put no more than 65 percent of their assets in equities at any one time—usually dividend-paying blue-chips like General Electric, Mobil, and AT&T (see table 5.2). The bonds they own are usually investment-grade.

Table 5.2

Balanced Funds

LARGEST HOLDINGS

Stock	Percent of Net Assets
Vanguard/Windsor II Fund	2.99%
General Electric	0.71
Vanguard/Windsor Fund	0.53
Mobil	0.43
AT&T	0.41
Vanguard U.S. Growth Fund	0.40
Exxon	0.39
E.I. Dupont de Nemours	0.38
May Department Stores	0.37
Pfizer	0.37

Also, half the major holdings of balanced funds are other mutual funds. For example, the $3.6 billion Vanguard STAR Fund, like the T. Rowe Price Spectrum funds, is a fund of funds. It creates a "balanced" portfolio by owning several other Vanguard funds, including Vanguard/Windsor, Vanguard/Windsor II, and Vanguard Fixed-Income's GNMA and Investment Grade portfolios.

The USAA Investment Cornerstone Fund follows a different tack. It takes five asset classes—U.S. stocks, U.S. bonds, real estate stocks, gold stocks, and foreign stocks—and tries to maintain a roughly equal weighting. The idea is intriguing for investors who would like to diversify across those asset classes. As a mutual fund investor, you could rebalance an array of funds just the way Cornerstone does. But do you have the discipline to do it?

Asset Allocation Funds

This type of fund didn't exist until the early 1980s, but there are now dozens, holding more than $20 billion in assets. These funds are different from balanced funds because they have no minimum or maximum allocations for stocks and bonds. While balanced funds usually keep equities at about 65 percent of the portfolio, an asset allocation fund manager can go to 100 percent *or* to 0 percent (or anything in between). That makes the asset allocation fund's results highly dependent on its manager's decisions.

In recent years, asset allocation funds have, on average, beat balanced funds; however, over specific 3-, 5-, and 10-year periods, balanced funds fared a little better.

Equities held by asset allocation funds tend to be many of the same big, dividend-paying blue-chips in the portfolios of moderate-risk growth-and-income, equity-income, and even balanced funds. But since many asset allocation funds count gold shares as an "asset class," one of the top holdings of asset allocation funds is American Barrick Resources, a gold producer.

Simply having a lot of latitude doesn't always produce greater returns for asset allocation fund shareholders. Some of these funds turn in lackluster performances year after year, and quite a few have disappeared entirely.

Though some of the asset allocation funds predate the 1987 market crash, many others opened for business in 1988. In their promotions they suggest to investors that their strategies can dodge market crashes. Given the wide latitude they have for investing, there will probably always be a few (like Dreyfus Capital Value) that will on occasion avoid market crashes. But remember: There's no evidence thus far that asset allocation funds can do any better for you than balanced funds.

International: Foreign, World, European, and Pacific Funds

The market values of U.S. stocks make up only about one-third of total world equity values, which is why U.S. investors are switching money to a new breed of mutual funds that makes it easy and convenient to invest abroad. Buying a portfolio of French, Brazilian, and Indonesian stocks is now no more difficult via mutual funds than buying a portfolio of U.S. blue-chips.

Of course, investing overseas is not a new idea. The Templeton Growth Fund, for instance, started investing in Japan during the 1950s when the notion that it would become the world's second-largest economy seemed absurd. Today most fund families have at least one international fund.

The busy trading floor of the Tokyo Stock Exchange

In fact, international funds have become such a diverse category that we've split the group into four, along geographic lines. *Foreign funds* invest *only* in non–U.S. stocks. *World funds* may invest in *both* foreign and U.S. stocks. The holdings look similar—such giants as Nestle, the Swiss-based food giant, and Hitachi, the Japanese electronics company. But two large holdings of world funds are also domestic: Merrill Lynch, the largest U.S. brokerage firm, and Federal National Mortgage Association, the quasi-government company that acts like a mortgage banker.

Whether these divisions make a difference depends on how you construct your portfolio. Suppose you want 25 percent of your total portfolio invested outside the United States. Go for foreign funds, since world funds may keep 40 or 50 percent of their assets in domestic stocks.

The areas where *European* and *Pacific funds* invest should be self-evident. These funds are not substitutes for other funds but are supplements, like sector funds for international equity.

Europe, for instance, is developing into one megamarket, with economic barriers falling rapidly. Eventually, this should make it nearly as easy for a Spanish company, for instance, to sell its products in France and Germany as it is now for a New Jersey company to sell in Pennsylvania and New York.

Pacific funds have some of the world's worst- and best-performing markets. The Japanese stock market was golden in the 1980s, especially for U.S. investors, but after 1990, the bear market in Japan was devastating for some Pacific funds.

The rest of Asia contains many other stories. Investing in Hong Kong, for example, poses huge risks. No one knows if Hong Kong will continue as the main doorway to China after it reverts to Chinese control in 1997. If not, foreigners might well pull out of the colony—and its stock market.

Some international funds invest in Latin American, and others in "emerging markets," such as Malaysia, Thailand, India, Africa, and Eastern Europe.

There's also a fundamental advantage to investing abroad. Spreading your assets over more markets raises potential rewards while lowering your portfolio's risk. When other countries are enjoying faster economic growth than the United States, corporate profits are going to be stronger there than here. By investing abroad you can capture some of that growth. You can also invest in industries that have all but disappeared in the United States, such as consumer electronics.

International funds have first-hand information on, say, Japanese banks or German machine-tool companies or Spanish utilities. Also, accounting standards and tax treatments vary across borders, so good equity analysis of non–U.S. companies requires specialized knowledge most U.S. investors just don't have. So even sophisticated investors frequently opt for mutual funds when investing abroad.

Not all international funds are managed in the same way. Many are "top-down" funds, focusing first on countries, their economies, growth prospects, and stock market valuations, and then allocating their assets between nations. Only then will fund managers choose stocks to fill the portfolios.

The Templeton funds, in contrast, buy from the bottom up, searching the globe for good investment opportunities at attractive prices and focusing first on companies, not countries.

The Oppenheimer Global Fund first identifies global investment themes, such as increased spending on infrastructure and telecommunications, and then looks for companies that may capitalize on them.

For some investors, the chief concern about international investing is currency risk: the chance that the value of your investments will change simply because of currency fluctuations. Is it worthwhile to take on currency risk if you're an American investing for retirement or college tuition payments? Yes, it is. Even with all your assets in dollars, you have some currency risk. When the dollar is falling in relation to other currencies, as it did through much of 1994, your European vacation may be prohibitively expensive, and you'll spend more dollars to buy foreign-made goods. You may also face higher prices for domestic goods, because higher prices for foreign cars, for example, may allow domestic car manufacturers to raise their prices, too. Putting a portion of your assets abroad is as American as baseball, hot dogs, apple pie, and Chevrolet.

Precious Metals Funds

Incredible. Astounding. Mind-boggling. No adjectives really do justice to the periodic performance of the funds specializing in precious metals, or gold funds. Lexington Strategic Investments, for example, has blasted out a 264.9 percent return in one year, probably close to an all-time record for a mutual fund! United Services Gold Shares has chalked up a 123.9 percent annual gain. In one recent year alone, the average gold fund delivered a whopping 97 percent return.

But in other years, Lexington Strategic Investments and the entire gold fund category did quite badly, as low as a 60.7 percent loss in one year. During the 1980s, an investor could have made as much money in a money-market mutual fund as in the average gold fund and without the risk.

So why invest in precious metals funds? The "safe haven" argument hasn't seemed very accurate in recent years, when gold stayed flat despite the Persian Gulf invasions and oil embargoes. Neither has the "inflation hedge" rationale, particularly when gold now moves up and down without much reference to the inflation rate.

One good reason to invest in precious metals funds is diversification. Most equity funds don't own any gold shares at all, so precious metals help your total portfolio do well in any

economic scenario. And the fluctuations in gold fund NAVs have little to do with any stock market indicator, further improving your portfolio's diversification and lowering your overall risk.

Specialty: Financial, Health-Care, Natural Resources, Technology, and Miscellaneous Funds

A specialty fund can behave like an index of stocks in a single industry or economic sector, like financial services. When the underlying sector does well, the fund can rise to the top.

For a few years, health-care funds led the performance derby followed next by financial funds, and, more recently, precious metals. (We've separated precious metals from the other specialty funds only because they have very different investment characteristics.)

If the fund managers do their jobs right, the specialty funds should have the same characteristics as the sectors of the stock market they represent. Natural resources funds primarily invest in energy and look best when energy prices are rising. Utilities funds buy stocks for their dividends, and should be very safe.

Obviously, specialty funds can perform only as well as the sectors in which they invest. The narrower a sector fund's mission, the more potential it has for big gains—*and* big losses. Despite the risks, specialty funds can provide a good alternative to stock picking in unpredictable industries. Select a single stock, and it can run into serious trouble with no advance warning. Specialty funds, however, own many stocks and are run by alert, sophisticated managers who may avoid problems you'd never spot in time.

Before you invest in specialty funds, keep a few things in mind: First, they have relatively short track records. The majority of these funds were formed in the 1980s. Also, many specialty funds are small, so expenses as a percentage of assets are high—often more than 2 percent right off the top of your returns.

Index and Social Investing Funds

Index funds are mutual funds designed to replicate, rather than beat, the performance of a certain market index. Most of the time index funds are easy to spot: either they have "index" in their title, or very low expenses, or both. They're low-cost because they simply follow an index, and thus can be managed largely by computers.

Index funds are popular because they're an easy way to match your returns to the index of your choice. In part, the index fund's edge comes from very low expenses, compared with other types of funds. Every point shaved from fund expenses winds up in investors' pockets. However, index funds that follow smaller, less efficient markets than the S&P 500 may provide less of a performance bonus because of higher transaction costs needed for the fund to mirror the index.

Also, index funds stay fully invested, so they follow indexes down in bear markets and do poorly. Managed funds can lighten up when stock prices decline, and therefore usually suffer a little less.

"Social investing" or "socially responsible" funds, like Dreyfus Third Century Fund and the Pax World Fund, don't invest in defense, tobacco, alcohol, or gaming industries. Even when an industry is socially okay, many of these funds screen companies for their labor relations, minority employment practices, environmental records, and attitudes toward women. Fixed-income socially responsible funds like Pax World won't invest in U.S. Treasury bonds because the proceeds could be used for military spending.

In recent years, some of the social investing funds have done well. Pax World and Dreyfus Third Century were top-rated funds for a while. This, however, doesn't mean social investing is a superior method of stock picking. It's just that in certain periods, certain industries that are naturals for social investing funds perform better than other investments. Social investing was never meant to enhance returns but instead to attempt to assure investors that their money wouldn't go to industries or practices they couldn't approve.

Closed-End Funds

These funds, whose format actually predates mutual funds by more than 100 years, offer professionally managed portfolios of securities and are regulated by the same laws as mutual funds. Many are even run by mutual fund management companies, and the returns from the best closed-end funds are much like the returns from regular mutual funds (see table 5.3).

The big difference between closed-end funds and regular mutual funds lies in how investors move their money in and out. When investors want to buy into a regular mutual fund, the fund management company issues new shares at the fund's NAV (plus a sales charge or "load" for certain funds). If the net asset value is $10 a share, for example, and you invest $10,000, you get 1,000 shares from the fund managers. When you want your money back, the fund management buys your shares at the prevailing net asset value. This arrange-

Table 5.3

Closed-End Bond Funds

BEST RETURNS

Period	Fund	Total Return*
1993	New America High Income	34.4%
1991–93	CIGNA High-Income	34.0
1989–93	Putnam High-Income Convertible	19.6
1984–93	Vestaur Securities	14.0

*Average annual, pretax

ment makes the mutual fund "open-ended."

Closed-end funds raise capital differently. A fund management company hires an investment bank, which organizes the underwriting and finds buyers for the soon-to-be-issued shares, just as for regular operating companies. The investment bank gets commitments from investors and sells the newly issued shares (the typical starting price is $10 each). If someone then wants to buy or sell shares in the closed-end fund after this initial underwriting is complete, he or she does so by trading, as with any stock: on any stock exchange.

Is this difference a big deal? It can be. Let's suppose that a closed-end fund's net asset value goes from $10 to $15. An investor may decide to take profits and ask a broker to sell the shares, but the broker may report back that the market price is only 13 1/2, or $13.50 a share. The portfolio is still worth $15, but, since the fund company won't redeem the shares, the only way the share owner can get cash for them is to find a buyer. And there's no law that a buyer has to pay NAV.

Closed-end equity funds typically sell at a discount to their underlying net asset value, a discount that in the past has been as high as 40 percent. With closed-end bond funds, discounts are smaller but can still remain in double digits. Immediately after their initial offerings, closed-end funds tend to trade at modest premiums to their net asset values, but within four to six months they're often trading at discounts. That's why most investment managers counsel investors never to buy initial offerings of closed-end funds.

Closed-End Yields

There are two ways for the fund's share price to go up. The first and most obvious way, of course, is through superior management. A winning portfolio will boost the net asset value, and that will tend to carry the fund's share price upward (though not necessarily dollar for dollar). The second way is for investors who missed the initial offering to bid up the shares on the market. But there won't be many investors doing this. With most closed-end funds, the size of the initial offering closely matches how much the brokers can sell. Sure, the underwriters might plan a $100 million offering, but if the sales force generates $300 million in orders, they'll boost the issue to match. Thus, nearly all the initial demand for a closed-end fund is met on the offering. Afterward, few investors who want to buy shares haven't already done so.

For a few months after the initial public offering, the investment bank that underwrote the fund usually buys enough shares to keep the price up. Sooner or later, however, the investment bank goes on to other business. When some of the original investors in the closed-end fund start to sell, there aren't many buyers for the shares. Prices begin to fall and eventually slip below NAV. Studies show that after four months the average discount for a domestic closed-end equity fund is 10.3 percent, and for a single-country equity fund, 11.4 percent. Closed-end bond funds seem to hold up better, trading at an average discount of only 0.12 percent.

Discount Funds

Fund managers don't spend money to promote existing closed-end funds, as they do with open-end funds, because new dollars in a mutual fund's portfolio will generate additional management fees. Closed-end funds, however, can't add new dollars to their portfolios, so managers have no incentive to bring in new investors.

(In recent years, many closed-end funds have raised additional capital through "rights" offerings, where existing shareholders are issued rights to buy new shares at a small discount to net asset value. If shareholders choose not to exercise these rights, they can sell them to other investors who may want to.)

Still, most fund managers today don't like to see their funds selling at big discounts to net asset value. Thus, many of the funds are now set up with provisions that allow them to buy back their own shares on the market if the discount widens to 10 percent—and often the ploy works. When a fund announces a share buyback, its shares often move up and may even trade at a slight premium.

Should the discounts prevail for too long, many funds have new provisions that allow shareholders to vote for conversion to an open-end structure. Once that happens, the discount disappears because investors can then take their money out at net asset value.

There's another wrinkle, too: A new sort of closed-end fund is in the works, known as the "interval" fund because it's designed to allow investors to redeem shares at predetermined intervals, such as once a month or a quarter. If existing closed-ends convert to this format, their discount/premium fluctuations should be minimized.

Long overshadowed by mutual funds, closed-end funds had a resurgence after the 1987 stock market crash. In fact, in 1989 closed-end single-country funds were 3 of the top 10 performers on the New York Stock Exchange. (The Asia Pacific Fund was No. 4; the Thai Fund, No. 5; the Germany Fund, No. 10.)

Some closed-end funds have traded up to enormous premiums, too.

Stockbrokers will remind you of this to aid their closed-end fund sales pitch. The Spain Fund at one time traded at 144.5 percent more than NAV—more than $24 for every $10 in assets. But such overvaluations don't last long. Less than a year later, the Spain Fund was trading at a 10 percent discount.

Shares of some single-country funds used to command premiums in the marketplace because they had a "franchise" that couldn't be duplicated, or because the underwriters couldn't satisfy all the demand for an issue. But most franchises have disappeared as competitive funds started up and as many emerging markets opened their doors to foreign investors.

Despite all the caveats about closed-end funds, they can be smart buys, especially when you might otherwise invest in a similar open-end fund (sometimes even run by the same fund manager). As portfolios, judge them by the same criteria.

Types of Closed-End Funds

Like the open-end mutual funds, the closed-end funds break down into equity and bond funds. Within those broad designations, there are nevertheless some differences. Only about one-third of the equity funds, for instance, are domestic funds investing in U.S. stocks. The rest of the equity funds are international funds broken down geographically: Europe, Latin America, Pacific, and world (see table 5.4). On the fixed-income side, there's corporate high-yield, corporate general, convertible government bond, and international bond as well as national and single-state muni bond funds.

There's another category that doesn't yet exist among the open-end funds: multisector bond funds. These funds attempt to allocate assets among various bond fund sectors, such as government, junk, and international, to maximize opportunities and lower the risk of investing in any one of those sectors.

Table 5.4

Closed-End Equity Funds

BEST RETURNS

Period	Fund	Total Return*
1993	Turkish Investment	151.6%
1991–93	First Financial	67.9
1989–93	Mexico	49.1
1984–93	Mexico	41.4

*Average annual, pretax

Since there are so many open-end funds with the same investment philosophies and approaches as closed-end funds, why bother with the closed-ends? One reason may be the discount. In fact, an investor who is bullish on a particular sector may do much better in the specialized closed-end fund than in an equivalent open-end portfolio, because the closed-end fund gives you more upside potential. Here's how:

Suppose you buy a health-care fund—with a NAV of $12—for $10 a share (in which case the fund is selling at nearly a 17 percent discount). If health-care stocks do well and the health-care portfolio climbs 20 percent, the net asset value of the closed-end fund is $14.40 ($12 plus 20 percent). If the fund still sells at a 17 percent discount, the fund would trade at $12.45. But investors might become more willing to bid for the closed-end fund, and the discount on the fund could narrow and perhaps disappear entirely! If the discount on your fund narrows to 5 percent, you'll get the portfolio's ordinary appreciation of 20 percent, which brings the NAV to $14.45, plus the lessening of the discount from 17 to 5 percent. That makes the selling price $13.68, a 36.8 percent return (before commissions) on your original $10 per share purchase price. An open-end health-care fund might have had the same 20 percent gain in its portfolio, but it cannot provide the extra gain from a decrease in its discount from NAV.

In a bull market this narrowing of the discount can give an investor in closed-end funds an extra edge. Of course, if the market turns down, that system can work the other way, increasing your losses. If the portfolio lost 20 percent of its value and the discount widened to 25 percent, the fund's $12 NAV would fall to $9.60 and, with the 25 percent discount, shares would sell at only $7.20, a 28 percent loss from your original investment.

Buying at Premium

Now let's look at what happens when you buy fund shares priced at a premium. Suppose you buy a fund on the initial offering for $10 a share. After underwriting fees and other miscellaneous expenses only $9.25 is left for NAV. So, in effect, you pay an 8 percent premium. Let's say the portfolio climbs 20 percent to $11.10 but, instead of a premium, the fund now sells at a 2 percent discount. If you sell, all you get is $10.87. So the portfolio went up 20 percent, but you receive less than 9 percent. Obviously, you're taking an extra risk if you buy closed-end funds selling at a premium to net asset value.

Because of differences between share price and NAV in closed-end funds, many fund investors choose to avoid them altogether. Nevertheless, there are times when closed-end funds can be the better buy.

Mario Gabelli, Charles Royce, and Martin Zweig are just a few of the many investment managers who run both closed- and open-end funds. If you're considering investing in one of their open-end funds, perhaps you should look at the comparable closed-end fund selling at a discount.

For instance, imagine an open-end fund and a closed-end fund with the same portfolio managers and many of the same stocks. They generally perform the same, but with the closed-end fund you can often get $1 worth of stock for 90 or 95 cents.

It's also possible to find bond funds trading at discounts to the NAV, but don't expect the same huge discounts you'll find in equity funds.

A good time to consider closed-end bond funds is when interest rates are falling. When short-term interest rates drop, investors seek to maintain their yields by pulling money out of money-market funds or CDs and buying long-term mutual bond funds. Such a strategy is often self-defeating. Money put into open-end funds during a time of falling interest rates will be invested at lower interest rates than the "older" money, lowering the average yield of the fund and diluting returns for all shareholders. Closed-end bond funds, because they don't take new money into the portfolio, don't suffer from dilution.

However, buying closed-end bond funds in a period of falling interest rates has some pitfalls, too. Since a falling-rate environment is a bull market for bonds, investors may bid up the market prices for closed-end bond funds, perhaps even trading them at a premium to net asset value.

There's a big difference between buying a bond at a premium and a bond fund at a premium. Bond fund "dividends" (they're technically dividends, even though the payout is earned from interest) can be cut, and often are, in a period of declining interest rates. Funds that don't cut, but still aren't earning enough to pay their dividends, can make a nontaxable distribution, which is a return of the investor's own capital. If you paid a premium for the bond fund, you lose during distributions because the money is paid out at the NAV.

Also watch out for high yields that are actually produced with lever-

Stock traders keeping track of the market's movement.

age. Here's how some investors might be lured in: Suppose the fund raises $200 million from investors for closed-end bond fund shares. The bond fund then sells another $100 million in preferred stocks—typically to corporations or other institutional investors. The preferred shares pay a dividend at either a fixed or a variable interest rate. This means the leveraged bond fund can invest $300 million instead of $200 million. If the fund can invest to produce an 8 percent interest rate while paying an average 5 percent rate on its preferred shares, the extra 3 percent on the extra $100 million can be paid out to common stockholders.

So far, so good. But what happens if the interest rates climb and bond prices tumble? The portfolio losses to the leveraged fund will be magnified. During the junk bond debacle of 1989 and 1990, junk bond funds that had leveraged their portfolios in this way were among the most heavily battered. In addition, if the rate on the preferred shares moves up higher than the interest payments on the bonds in the portfolio, the bond fund might have to pay the preferred shareholders their extra from the common shareholders' capital.

The moral of the story: If a closed-end bond fund seems to promise a return that's higher than what the market bears, look carefully to see *how* the fund is producing it.

Convertible Funds

In the motor world, convertibles are peppy and flashy cars, but in the mutual fund world, they've often been sluggish performers, never quite firing on all cylinders.

Convertible bonds are simply bonds that, in addition to paying interest, give investors the ability to swap them for a specified amount of stock in the issuing company. Because of the convertibility feature, their interest rates are lower than they would otherwise be. But the bonds should be steadier than common stock, since they pay more interest than the stock's dividend (some convertible-bond issuers pay no dividends at all on their stock).

In theory, convertible bonds—and convertible bond funds—provide the investor much of the comfort of owning a fixed-income security, but with an opportunity to garner some capital gains if the company's stock rises. The practical experience with convertible bond funds, however, has been a different story. True, in some years convertible funds trounce the Lehman Brothers' Government/Corporate Bond Index and the Standard & Poor's 500. But in other years, convertibles lag both stocks and bonds.

The problem is that about two-thirds of all convertibles are junk bonds, suffering from the same problems and worries that plague the high-yield market. Blue-chip companies usually don't need to issue convertibles since they can issue regular bonds at favorable rates. More than 60 percent of convertible bonds are issued by companies with a market value of $1 billion or less. However, some better-quality issuers have recently begun to issue convertibles. The convertible funds that have fared the best have stayed nimble and have steered away from the worst of the junk.

When market conditions are right, some funds create "synthetic convertibles" by pairing straight debt and call options on the issuer's stock (it's effectively the very same thing). Other convertible bond funds just park their money in straight debt or equity when they don't like what's happening in the convertibles market.

Government Mortgage Funds

Name plates don't always tell the whole story of a mutual fund. Consider the giant Franklin U.S. Government Securities Fund. The name doesn't tell you that it's primarily invested in mortgage-backed securities. Many such funds don't put "mortgage" in their names. Are they trying to pull a fast one on you? Not exactly.

Mortgage funds fall under the "government" category because most mortgage-backed securities are created by government or government-related agencies. This includes the Federal National Mortgage Association (or "Fannie Mae"), the Federal Home Loan Mortgage Corporation ("Freddie Mac"), and the Government National Mortgage Association ("Ginnie Mae"). Most mortgage funds hold some plain Treasury securities, too. The purpose of slapping "U.S. Government" on the fund is to reassure investors.

The mortgage-backed securities provide more yield than plain Treasury bonds, but not always more total return. During a period of falling interest rates, mortgage funds can do well, but usually not as well as plain Treasury funds. Mortgage securities are often paid off prematurely when interest rates fall as homeowners rush to refinance mortgages at the new, lower rates.

To understand how mortgage securities work, think of your own situation. Most of these funds invest in

Table 5.5

Convertible Bond Funds

BEST RETURNS

Period	Fund	Total Return*
1993	Pacific Horizon Capital Income	20.2%
1991–93	Pacific Horizon Capital Income	26.3
1989–93	Pacific Horizon Capital Income	19.6

*Average annual, pretax

Table 5.6

Government — Mortgage Funds

BEST RETURNS

Period	Fund	Total Return*
1993	Alliance Mortg. Secs. Income B	9.4%
1991-93	Princor Government Secs. Income	10.6
1989-93	Vanguard Fixed-Income GNMA	10.8

*Average annual, pretax

home mortgages, just like yours. You make a mortgage payment every month to a bank, thrift, or mortgage company. Of course, you don't send your payment to a mutual fund. But it's likely that the original lender has sold your mortgage and is now merely collecting payments and forwarding the proceeds—less a small service charge, of course. Your mortgage, along with hundreds of others, is pooled together into a mortgage-backed security—the type of investment that is the principal holding of the government-mortgage funds.

Who Buys Mortgage Funds?

Mutual funds are among the major buyers of mortgage-backed securities. In that sense, they have a role to play in supporting home ownership. You may even invest in the mutual fund that owns the security that includes your mortgage. Fannie Mae's, Freddie Mac's, and Ginnie Mae's mortgage-backed securities are prized by investors, since their credit quality is considered just a shade under that of pure Treasury securities. If borrowers default, the federal agencies guarantee interest and principal, and the federal government stands behind the agencies. Yet the yields are about one percentage point higher than Treasury bonds.

Some mortgage-backed securities are bonds, with pools of mortgages serving as collateral. Many are mortgage pass-through certificates, like owning the mortgages themselves. A growing segment of this market is collateralized mortgage obligations, better known as CMOs. These are about the most complex instruments a mutual fund can own. Like mortgage pass-throughs, CMOs are securities backed by a pool of mortgages. But holders of pass-through securities, like holders of GNMAs, receive equal shares of all interest payments and prepayments. CMOs, instead, carve up the income and principal payments from an underlying pool of mortgages in special ways. Some investors receive interest only (IOs); some receive principal-only payments (POs). Some pay off early and predictably; others are subject to wild fluctuation.

Even big Wall Street trading houses trip up on IOs and POs and find themselves with large, embarrassing trading losses. The rules that apply to all fixed-income investing also apply here. When interest rates go up, the value of existing mortgages goes down. There's another dynamic at work, too. The interest, and a small part of the principal, is paid monthly and is predictable. But mortgagors can pay off their principal at any time. A certain amount of prepayment is always figured into the price of a mortgage security.

But what is unsettling to the mortgage market—and to funds that invest in mortgage securities—is sudden changes in expectations about principal repayment. Here's why: The mortgage-backed market operates on the assumption that a pool of mortgages will have an "average life" of 12 years, mainly because most people move or refinance their homes well before they pay off a mortgage. But a change in interest rates also alters the expected life of a mortgage-backed security. If that life expectancy drops to 10 years—or lengthens to 15 years—the price of the securities can change dramatically.

Here's an example: Suppose you buy a house and finance the deal with a 9 percent mortgage, which, in turn, is owned by investors through a mortgage-backed security with a 9 percent coupon. Five years go by and you're ready to move, but interest rates shoot up to 11 percent. You can't sell your house, because the higher interest rates have depressed the housing market. In addition, you're reluctant to take on a mortgage at 11 percent.

Instead of selling your home and paying back the mortgage, you stay in the house for a few more years. At the same time, the investors who hold your mortgage are also hurt because, like all fixed-income instruments, the higher interest rate lowers its value. And because you and many others will be holding on to your 9 percent mortgages longer, the security now has a 15-year expected life. Higher rates and a longer life make the security less desirable.

Suppose, instead, that interest rates had dropped to 7 percent. The owners of your mortgage would be happy, because they're getting 9 percent from you while new mortgages are fetching only 7 percent. But you're likely to sell your house and pay off the 9 percent mortgage, or refinance to take advantage of the 7 percent rate. That means the investors receive principal repayments faster than originally expected, and the security with a 12-year life expectancy now looks like a 10-year. If rates were going up, the mortgage holders would like the faster payback, but with rates heading down, the last thing they want is principal coming back to them. Principal that was earning 9 percent must now be reinvested at only 7 percent. As mortgage rates came down a few years ago, one of the major problems for mortgage-fund managers was minimizing prepayment risks.

Market Influences

Just how good mortgage funds are as investments depends on other market conditions. On the one hand, high-coupon mortgage securities usually lag behind bond market rallies because investors are reluctant to pay more for high-yielding mortgages when conditions are ripe for homeowners to pay them off. On the other hand, when bonds begin to falter, mortgages often hold up better because the principal which does come back gets reinvested at higher rates. Held over an "interest-rate cycle"—a period when rates go up, down, and then return to the starting point—the mortgage funds should outperform the pure Treasury funds by about one percentage point a year.

Not all government mortgage funds are alike, however. Franklin U.S. Government Securities and Vanguard Fixed-Income GNMA, the two largest funds in this category, buy simple GNMA securities, steering clear of the exotic mortgage-backed products. In contrast, Alliance Mortgage Securities Income Fund has successfully gone beyond GNMAs and, so far, has avoided much of the pain of prepayments (see table 5.6). The Alliance funds practice a strategy called "dollar roll," selling securities "forward" (usually to dealers) with an agreement to buy them back within 30 or 60 days. Those who buy the securities bear the risk of interest prepayments during the time they own them. The funds, meanwhile, reinvest the proceeds of these sales in safe short-term securities with negligible risks.

Government Adjustable Rate Mortgage Funds (ARMs)

Every time interest rates fall, yield-conscious investors panic. How will they get more interest without more risk? Fund management companies and brokers who sell funds work to come up with the "magic bullet" investment to do just that. Until recently, many investors and fund managers thought they had found a gem in adjustable-rate mortgage ("ARM") funds. Like other mortgage funds, most of the securities in these portfolios have the backing of federal agencies. Credit quality is pristine. But conventional mortgage funds own fixed-rate mortgage-backed securities, so rising interest rates pose a risk of principal loss.

The interest rates on ARMs change, eliminating some of that risk; however, the changes occur not in lockstep with the general level of rates but semiannually or annually, depending on the mortgages. So an ARM that resets its interest rate yearly should behave much like a one-year bond. The risk of losing principal on a one-year security is negligible—or so the sales pitch goes. But investors in ARM funds found that there's much more at risk than they were initially led to believe.

Yields and Risks

Because ARM securities have higher yields than, say, short-term Treasuries, they typically sell at a premium. So an ARM with a 6 percent yield may sell for $1,050, or 105 in bond parlance. But then interest rates go down, and at the next reset the yield falls to 5 percent. Now the ARM may sell for only $1,030, or 103. The fund's shareholders lose that $20 out of net asset value. Analysts say the yields advertised by ARM funds are often misleading because they don't take this downward bias into account. Some fund companies openly voice their concerns about this problem: T. Rowe Price Adjustable Rate U.S. Government Fund, for instance, warns shareholders to expect a four-cent decline in NAV each year. Still, T. Rowe Price says the fund makes good investment sense because it has the potential to deliver an extra two percentage points in yield.

But that's not the only problem posed by the ARM funds. Like conventional mortgage funds, falling rates often encourage homeowners to refinance. ARMs purchased at 103 or 105 are paid off at 100. Fund shareholders have to eat these losses, too. And there's more. To boost yield, fund managers may invest as much as a third of the portfolio in other than government-sponsored ARMs. These securities, such as interest-only payments (IOs), are more risky than conventional ARMs. If prepayments increase, IOs fall in price because the interest rate on a paid-off mortgage is zero.

Although ARMs funds are not a magic bullet, they can offer a decent return with a modest amount of risk. Whether they delight or disappoint the investor depends on expectations. Investors concerned about NAV stability should seek out the "purest" ARM funds they can find—those that invest in government-backed ARMs—and stay clear of those that dabble in other securities.

The other caveat, which applies to all funds but especially low-yield ones, is to watch out for high loads and expense fees. Every additional tenth of a percentage point that goes to pay a salesperson or a fund manager is money that would otherwise go to the investor.

Chapter 6

Buying and Selling: The Essentials

At any brokerage firm you can buy or sell just about any stock or bond—but not all mutual funds. Brokers sell plenty of mutual funds and, in fact, account for more than half of all fund sales. But not all brokers sell all funds. The major brokerage firms sell the wares of fund companies such as Alliance Capital, Franklin, Putnam, and Templeton. Only about half the brokers' fund sales go to such outside managers; the rest go to their own in-house funds. But they certainly don't sell their competitors' products, so don't expect a Merrill Lynch broker to help you buy a PaineWebber mutual fund. If you don't know where to buy the broker-sold fund you want, call the fund's toll-free number and ask.

You can't get funds like T. Rowe Price, Scudder, Janus, or Vanguard through most brokers. (Several discount brokerage firms handle them, however. More about this later.) These fund companies sell direct to investors, mainly through the mail, toll-free telephone lines, and, in some cases, walk-in offices. But they are worlds unto themselves, as are the funds managed by any single company.

Switching from T. Rowe Price New Horizons Fund to T. Rowe Price New Income Fund or T. Rowe Price Growth & Income Fund, or between any two funds managed by the same company, is a snap. You can do it via a telephone over a toll-free line. But if you're bailing out of New Horizons to invest in the Janus Fund, you have to ask for a check from T. Rowe Price, then mail it to Janus. The process can go a little faster if you've arranged for bank wire transfers, but the burden is still on *you* to handle the transaction.

What You Need to Know about Loads

For most of their history, mutual funds were sold by salespeople working for the fund companies, brokerage firms, and insurance companies. Funds usually came with a stiff "load," or commission charge paid by the investors. Today, this is still true of most funds sold by brokers.

For many years the load was an 8.5 percent up-front sales charge that lopped a big chunk of money off the top of your investment. Out of every $1,000, $85 would go toward commissions and only $915 into investments. The 8.5 percent charge usually applied to investments of less than $10,000. For larger amounts, the percentage would scale back and might even disappear at, say, $1 million. Though the regulators kept it a tad lower than the initial front-end load, a few fund managers also levied a load on your reinvested dividends and capital gains. Some still do. If the commission seemed high, salespeople would remind investors that, unlike stocks and bonds, it was paid only on purchase—not when you sold.

Today, not all funds charge this "load" to investors. Still, there are many more load than no-load funds, because many funds need brokers to bring in investors. Some no-loads with excellent track records never attracted many investors—until they added loads and began paying brokers to sell them. The first year AIM Weingarten was a load fund, assets under management increased by about $98 million, or 58 percent. The Pasadena Growth Fund switched from no-load to a 3 percent load, and when this proved too small to get the brokers excited about the fund, the load was boosted to 5.5 percent. Sales took off, and the fund more than doubled its assets in less than a year.

A few years ago, mutual fund regulators on the U.S. Securities & Exchange Commission staff proposed negotiated loads, allowing fund companies, brokers, and investors to dicker over price. After all, stock commissions have been negotiable since 1975—why not funds? The fund industry howled, and the SEC commissioners didn't press it. The matter quickly died.

No-Load Funds

In the early 1970s, the stock market plummeted, and so did mutual fund sales. To shake off the slump, some mutual fund companies started to sell direct to investors without a sales charge. The idea for no-load funds wasn't brand new, even then. The earliest no-loads were started by investment counseling firms like T. Rowe Price for accounts deemed too small for individual management and were not widely marketed. When the no-loads were coupled with liberalized rules on mutual fund advertising, however, they did very well. Fund management companies like Dreyfus and Fidelity saw the light: They began dropping the loads from some of their funds and launching new funds without loads.

Money-market funds were also sold no-load and drew millions of new investors into mutual funds in the 1970s. Their popularity worked to the advantage of the mutual fund companies with no-load funds.

Until the mid-1980s, the mutual fund universe was split between the load funds, with their 8.5 percent sales charges, and the no-loads. Then the load funds, feeling investor resistance to the stiff fees, started lowering their sales charges. Now only a handful of fund groups charge 8.5 percent. Most have dropped their fees to between 4 and 6 percent. Increasingly, they have also a different payment plan—the "back-end" load.

Back-End Loads

Back-end loads are also called "redemption fees," "exit fees," or, technically, "contingent deferred sales charges." The fee is set to decline the longer you hold the fund. If you sell your shares in the first year, you pay the full charge, perhaps 4 or 5 percent. If you sell in the second year, your exit fee is reduced by one percentage point, and so on. By the fifth or sixth year the redemption fee is gone, so long-term investors never pay it.

Back-end loads were first introduced about a decade ago, but this alternative didn't really become popular until the late 1980s, when Merrill Lynch introduced "dual pricing." Dual pricing creates two classes of shares for each fund: "A" shares carry a one-time up-front load, and "B" shares carry the back-end load. Dual pricing is now widespread among both the brokerage house funds and even the independent fund managers who sell through brokers. While many use the A and B share method, Kemper and a few others offer a separate lineup of funds with back-end loads.

During the 1980s, as the load funds lowered up-front sales charges and introduced back-end loads, some no-load companies were going the opposite way. Fidelity Investments, for instance, slapped "low-loads"—2 or 3 percent sales charges—on funds that were previously no-loads. Fidelity then used the load to pay for its extensive advertising.

By the 1990s, the mutual fund industry enjoyed record sales, but investors were resisting loads. Strong Funds, which had low-loads on its equity funds, dropped them altogether. Fidelity began waiving its low-loads on most funds (except Magellan and Select Portfolios) purchased in retirement accounts.

In recent years, some load funds with good track records, such as Oberweis Emerging Growth, switched to no-load, and Heartland Value Fund switched its front-end load to a back-end load.

Nevertheless, you may be required to pay fees even for no-load funds. For instance, the Vanguard Group levies a 1 percent "transaction fee" on its index funds. The difference between this fee and most loads is that the proceeds go to the fund rather than the fund management company. The fee is used to offset the transaction costs of investing the money. (In most funds, this cost is reflected in the price that a fund pays for securities.)

The Vanguard index funds levy a $2.50 per quarter "maintenance fee" on investors to cover the costs of reports, statements, and the like. In most funds, these costs end up on the line itemized as "other expenses."

Some no-loads charge redemption fees, too, but usually to discourage short-term trading. Vanguard charges 1 percent on redemptions of its Specialized Portfolio series of funds. The Lindner Fund and the Lindner Dividend Fund take a 2 percent redemption fee on shares sold within 60 days of purchase. The Pennsylvania Mutual Fund levies a 1 percent exit fee on shares redeemed within a year of purchase.

Table 6.1

The Biggest Fund Managers and How They Sell Their Wares

Fund Management Company	Assets Billions*	Direct Sales No-load, Low-load, and Institutional	Sales Force Load and Deferred
Fidelity	$231.3	•	•
Merrill Lynch	126.7		•
Vanguard	125.7	•	
Franklin/Templeton	93.8		•
Capitol Research	93.8		•
Dreyfus	72.6	•	•
Dean Witter	66.1		•
Putnam	59.5		•
Federated	50.5	•	
Kemper	45.7		•
Smith Barney Shearson	56.4		•
Prudential	41.6		•
IDS	36.5		•
Scudder	35.7	•	
T. Rowe Price	34.7	•	
Nuveen	32.7		•
Alliance Capital	27.9		•
MFS	26.2		•
Oppenheimer	25.7		•
PaineWebber	25.4		•
AIM Management	24.7		•
20th Century	23.4	•	
Provident Institutional	22.1		•
Goldman, Sachs	22.0	•	•
Bank of America	18.1		•

*As of Dec. 31, 1993. Excludes variable annuities and off-shore funds

Since the subtleties of loads and other charges have so muddled the distinction between load and no-loads funds, the terms don't mean so much these days. In fact, the Investment Company Institute, the mutual fund industry's trade association, categorizes funds by the method used to distribute them, not by the sales charges. They list "sales force" funds—those sold to investors through sales people—and "direct marketing" funds—those sold by the management companies direct to investors (see table 6.1).

Hidden Loads

If the differences between loads, low-loads, and no-loads aren't confusing enough, consider the "12(b)-1" fee, often called the "hidden load."

The 12(b)-1 charge, named for the U.S. Securities & Exchange Commission rule which enabled funds to levy it, is meant to help funds defray marketing and distribution costs, just like loads. Sales-force fund companies can use the 12(b)-1 revenues to compensate brokers for their selling efforts. Direct marketing companies often use the money to pay for advertising. At least half of all funds levy some sort of 12(b)-1 fee.

What's very different about this charge is how it is collected from the fund's shareholders. Instead of paying the charge once when they buy the fund (front-end load), or when they sell it (back-end load), investors pay this fee by having it deducted from the fund's assets. In this sense, the 12(b)-1 charges are like the fees shareholders pay for portfolio management, administration, auditing, printing, postage, and other miscellaneous expenses.

There are regulatory limits on 12(b)-1 fees. The fee—which must be disclosed in the prospectus—cannot exceed 0.75 percent of assets per year, or 75 cents per $100 of assets, plus a 0.25 percent "service fee," for a total of 1 percent. Many funds, in fact, charge less. Many sales-force fund companies with front-end loads also offer funds with back-end loads and 12(b)-1 fees. Many no-load funds also charge 12(b)-1 fees but are usually smaller than sales-force funds. The rules say a fund that calls itself "no load" can charge 12(b)-1 fees of no more than 0.25 percent.

One percent may not sound like much, but on a $10,000 investment, that's $100 per year. And when the fund is increasing in value, that 1 percent not only represents more money each year but also money that is no longer yours to compound annually.

Rules enacted in 1992 are designed to cap 12(b)-1 fees so investors don't pay more than they would have paid on an 8.5 percent load. The cap, however, pertains to the entire fund and not to any individual investor. According to experts, the 12(b)-1 fee on a fund that is not growing would eventually hit the cap, while a fund that's taking in new money may never hit its cap, forcing investors to pay the 12(b)-1 fee indefinitely.

Confusing enough? It's getting worse.

Alliance Capital has A, B, and C versions for all its stock and bond funds. The A shares carry a 4.5 percent front-end load. The B shares have an ongoing 1 percent annual 12(b)-1 charge plus a declining back-end load. For equity funds, the back-end load is 4 percent in the first year, declining one percentage point a year, and disappearing in the fifth year. For fixed-income funds, the back-end load starts at 3 percent and disappears in the fourth year. The C shares charge neither front- nor back-end loads—just a 1 percent per year fee, sometimes called a "level load." Like the 12(b)-1 fee, the level load comes out of the fund's assets.

Where will mutual fund pricing schemes end? Well, mutual fund companies are always coming up with new ways to sell mutual funds. One of the latest is the "hub and spoke" or "master and feeder" fund arrangement. It works like this: A fund company sets up and manages, for example, a government bond fund. That's the hub. Since this company distributes directly to individual investors, it opens a no-load government bond fund, a spoke. Instead of owning government bonds, the spoke fund owns shares in the hub fund, which owns the government bonds. Next, the fund company thinks banks might want to sell this government bond fund to their customers, so it creates another spoke, perhaps with the bank's name on it, and sells it with a load. The company can go on and on, creating new spokes for sales through different distribution channels—institutional investors, retirement plans, and offshore investors—all owning shares in the same hub.

One advantage of this arrangement is that it's cheaper to operate one large, centralized hub portfolio than several smaller funds. These savings should be passed on to investors as lower expenses, but that doesn't always happen. Investors may not even realize that their fund is the spoke of a hub, and if they're satisfied with results they may not care. But suppose you paid a load to invest in a spoke fund, while others bought spokes into the same hub for a lesser load, or even no load. You'd be at a disadvantage, and you might become angry. According to current regulations, a broker selling you a spoke fund has no obligation to tell you there's another spoke of the same hub with a different pricing scheme. It's up to *you* to ask.

Loads, low-loads, and hidden loads cost you money and can be confusing. Should you forgo all of them and just concentrate on no-load funds? Not necessarily. As long as you understand the sales charges, exit fees, and ongoing distribution fees and how they affect the total return from your investment, you might easily prefer a fund with some sort of load to a comparable no-load fund.

The Securities & Exchange Commission, for the most part, has been fairly vigilant on fee disclosure. Its philosophy has been to provide investors with all the information—and let the buyer decide.

To Load or Not to Load?

Why would anyone buy a load fund when, in most cases, you can find a no-load analog to any load fund?

Since portfolio performance has nothing to do with whether you paid a broker to sell you the fund, you might as well buy no-loads, right? Perhaps. That's a question only you can answer for yourself.

You may want to take these decisions into your own hands, instead of using a broker or financial planner. But it's a mistake to dismiss load funds entirely, because you're cutting yourself off from a large part of the mutual fund universe and many excellent investment opportunities.

When the only alternative to no-load funds was an 8.5 percent load, the scales tipped heavily toward the no-loads. Today, however, there are funds with 2 and 3 percent low-loads, funds with 4 percent loads, and funds with back-end loads, which many investors never have to pay.

In determining whether to pay a load, consider how long you anticipate staying with the fund. Everyone's financial plans are subject to change, of course, but if you're thinking about a one- or two-year investment, do you really want to pay a load?

However, if your investment is for your retirement nest egg or your toddler's college education, a load should not stand between you and the best possible fund. After all, even an 8.5 percent load—and there are few of them remaining—over a 10-year holding period works out to less than 1 percent per year. That kind of sales burden can easily be overcome by the performance of an exceptional fund versus a mediocre one.

An additional consideration is that, even if your investment goal or your ability to tolerate risk changes, all is not lost. Most load-fund families, just like no-loads, have a wide range of portfolios to choose from, and intrafamily switches, such as moving from a Putnam International Bond Fund to a Putnam Government Bond Fund, can usually be done without paying another load. Increasingly, some load fund groups like Fortis and Prudential permit investors to switch funds out of other load funds and into theirs without paying a new load.

What about A, B, and C shares offered by Alliance Capital? (Remember, as discussed earlier in this chapter, that the A shares have a sales charge of 4.5 percent plus a 0.3 percent 12(b)-1 fee, the B shares, a 1 percent 12(b)-1 fee and a declining redemption fee of 4 percent in the first

When interested in long-term saving—for a child's college education, or retirement—even a fund with a large load can overcome a mediocre no-load fund.

year, 3 in the second, right down to zero by the fifth year, and the C shares have no entry or exit fee but charge 1 percent per year.) Suppose you're investing $10,000 and hope to earn, on average, 10 percent a year. Which shares—A, B, or C—will maximize your return? If there's a chance you'll have to redeem the shares in the first or second year, the B and C shares are better. At that point, the A shares would be worth $12,744, and the B and C shares, $12,915. If you redeem B shares at that point, you pay a 3 percent back-end load, so your B share proceeds drop to $12,577, making the C shares a better deal. But in the fourth year and beyond, the A shares fare best.

If B and C deliver the same investment results, why would anyone agree to the B shares with their back-end loads? Easy. After 8 years, Alliance converts the B shares into A shares which have no back-end load and a lower 12(b)-1 fee. The C shares pay the 1 percent annual load forever. If you plan to stay in the fund for 10 or 20 years, C shares can cost you an enormous amount of money. Not all fund companies with multiple classes of shares offer this delayed conversion privilege, so if you're thinking about investing in B shares, it pays to seek out a company that does.

In weighing a load versus a no-load fund, you should also consider the fund's investment parameters. For instance, equity funds generally have broad charters and often disparate results. So even if both funds are going for growth, the difference in returns can be great, and having the "right" fund can be extra profitable. Paying a modest load for an equity fund with demonstrated superior results can be better than buying an inferior no-load. However, short-term bond funds all maintain a fairly similar portfolio, and there are few differences in returns from one fund to another. Therefore, it doesn't make sense to pay a load for a short-term bond fund when there's little likelihood it will show better performance than a comparable no-load fund.

There is at least one other reason to pay a load: to compensate a broker or financial planner for the time he or she spends meeting with you and monitoring your investments. Perhaps a recommendation for one equity fund does not merit paying a 6 percent load. That's *your* decision. But if a financial planner takes the time to tailor a portfolio of funds for you, he or she ought to be paid, and the load is one way to do it. There are other ways as well. Some financial planners, for instance, put their clients' money into no-load funds and then levy an annual fee, perhaps 1 or 2 percent, on the entire portfolio. That's not necessarily a better deal for investors. If you are investing for more than a few years, you might be better off paying your planner by investing in quality load funds.

Six percent off the top of your initial investment may sound steep, but fund managers slicing off 1 percent a year for 10 years take more than you'd give up with a 9.5 percent initial load.

Keep in mind, too, that while it's common practice to refer to a fund as a "4 percent load" or an "8.5 percent load," not everyone pays the full freight. Most load funds have fee schedules that slide downward for progressively larger investments. Typically, purchases up to $10,000 carry the maximum load. Before making an investment in a load fund, ask the broker about the dollar amount necessary to qualify for a lower load. In some cases, it might be worth putting in an extra $1,000 or $2,000 to shave the load a bit.

You may not even have to come up with all the cash at one time. Suppose you plan to invest $15,000 but won't be able to put in all the money at once. See if the fund management company will let you sign a letter of intent, pledging to invest over a certain period a specified amount which, if invested at one time, would qualify for a reduced sales charge. If you fail to fulfill the letter of intent, you'll owe the extra sales charge.

If you're spreading your investments over several funds in the same load fund group, see if you can get the same break as if you made the investment in just one fund.

Prospecting the Prospectus

Let's face it. Nobody wants to read a prospectus. It's a document written in legal and financial terms that sound awfully technical—but the language is precise for a reason. The SEC has strict guidelines about what a fund can say about itself and how it must present information on past performance, expenses, and fees.

The SEC's approval of a prospectus is not an endorsement of any particular investment, just an acknowledgment that the prospectus itself complies with applicable laws. It's still up to *you* to read, understand, and interpret what it says.

Prospectuses may look daunting today, but they're far more comprehensible than just a few years ago. Today they are simpler to read with easier-to-compare figures and a lot less bulk. They contain most of the objective information you need: sales charges and fees, investment policy, and administrative matters like the procedure for redeeming shares or switching into other funds. If the fund has an operating history, the prospectus provides that, too. What the prospectus won't have is a glowing recommendation from a sales rep or a complimentary article from a financial publication. That's in the sales literature stuffed into the same envelope.

There's a good chance that prospectuses may get slimmer yet. The SEC is considering whether to approve the "summary prospectus" or a "prospectus on a page." This would enable mutual funds to incorporate critical prospectus information into their advertising. Currently, an investor who likes a mutual fund has to receive a prospectus before investing. Under the newly proposed SEC guidelines, investors would be able to clip an application off an advertisement that contains the summary prospectus and send it in with a check immediately. This plan, known in the industry as "off the page sales," would level the playing field for the direct-sales fund companies, allowing them to deliver a full prospectus along with a confirmation statement—just like the broker-sold funds can do right now.

Statement of Additional Information (SAI)

This bulkier presentation is more of what prospectuses used to be. It covers the same ground but in far more detail. For instance, in a recent year the prospectus for the Scudder Short-Term Bond Fund was a manageable 20 pages, measuring 7 1/4 x 8 1/4 inches. That's about par for a mutual fund prospectus. The Statement of Additional Information for the same fund was 60 pages, 8 1/2 x 11 inches.

In one paragraph, the prospectus said the fund could invest in, among other things, high-quality mortgage-backed securities. The SAI went on for four pages about various sorts of mortgage-backed securities and how they work.

For most investors, the prospectus will suffice. Although it is unlikely that you will ever need to review the SAI, it's important to be aware that it exists. In a landmark case decided in a federal appellate court in New York, an investor challenged a fee that he claimed was nonexistent in the prospectus. The judges ruled that investors are responsible for knowing what's in the Statement of Additional Information and, since the existence of the SAI was noted in the prospectus and the SAI discussed the fee, the court ruled that the investor could not claim he was unaware of it.

State securities administrators who oversee the activities of securities firms at the state level have been urging fund investors to request SAIs and appealing to the SEC to require more detailed information in the prospectuses so investors don't have to read both documents. The SEC's Division of Investment Management, which regulates mutual funds, has resisted any moves that might fatten up the prospectuses. If the prospectus is a rarely read document now, it will be even less so if it becomes thicker and thus more detailed and cumbersome.

Taking a Closer Look

Don't let the prospectus unnerve you. The financial matters and investment policies may be unique to a particular fund, but much of the other material is boilerplate and doesn't vary much from one fund to another. What's more, not all of it is pertinent to every investor. For example, as long as your planned investment isn't for your Individual Retirement Account or other tax-deferred program, you don't need to read the IRA section in the prospectus.

When thumbing through the prospectus, look for important statistical nuggets like the fund's results and expenses. These documents plainly outline all sales charges, deferred sales charges, redemption fees, exchange fees, management fees, 12(b)-1 fees, and other pertinent expenses. There will also be a condensed financial history of the fund. (Most of these data are also available from other sources.)

Want to take a closer look? Examine tables 6.2 and 6.3 from a recent Fidelity Magellan Fund prospectus. Look at the expense summary. You can see the maximum sales charge, 3 percent. The introductory note tells you on what pages you can find more detailed information on the sales charge. For instance, under certain circumstances, the sales charge can be waived. You can also see in plain language that there is no sales charge on reinvested dividends, and no deferred sales charges or fees for exchanges (that is, moving money from fund to fund within a family of funds).

Then come the operating expenses. The introductory note explains what goes into the charges. The management fee, which can vary depending on the fund's performance, is estimated to be 0.75 percent, or 75 cents per $100 of assets. Other expenses, which include such administrative costs as maintaining shareholder records and furnishing reports and financial statements, amounts to another 0.25 percent. If

Table 6.2

Financial History

This information has been audited by Coopers & Lybrand, independent accountants. Their unqualified report is included in the fund's Annual Report. The Annual Report is incorporated by reference into (is legally a part of) the Statement of Additional Information.

Per-Share Data										
Fiscal years ended March 31	1984	1985	1986	1987	1988	1989	1990	1991	1992	**1993**
Investment income	$.63	$1.11	$.76	$.81	$1.17	$1.64	$1.90	$1.98	$1.35	**$1.77**
Expenses	.26	.32	.27	.39	.54	.55	.55	.59	.54	**.57**
Net investment income	.37	.79	.49	.42	.63	1.09	1.35	1.39	.81	**1.20**
Distributions from net investment income	(.26)	(.37)	(.65)	(.46)	(.72)	(.90)	(1.24)	(.83)	(1.30)	**(1.25)**
Net realized & unrealized gain (loss) on investments	2.73	5.75	19.59	11.39	(6.64)	8.63	9.39	8.10	9.21	**9.18**
Distributions from net realized gain on investments	(1.88)	(3.69)	(1.78)	(6.84)	(9.02)	—	(3.82)	(2.42)	(5.43)	**(8.82)**
Net increase (decrease) in net asset value	.96	2.48	17.65	4.51	(15.75)	8.82	5.68	6.24	3.29	**.31**
Net asset value **(NAV)** beginning of year	34.25	35.21	37.69	55.34	59.85	44.10	52.92	58.60	64.84	**68.13**
Net asset value at end of year	$35.21	$37.69	$55.34	$59.85	$44.10	$52.92	$58.60	$64.84	$68.13	**$68.44**
Ratios										
Ratio of net investment income to average net assets	1.47%	2.79%	1.95%	1.18%	1.33%	2.13%	2.54%	2.47%	1.57%	**2.11%**
Ratio of expenses to average net assets	1.04%	1.12%	1.08%	1.08%	1.14%	1.08%	1.03%	1.06%	1.05%	**1.00%**
Ratio of management fee to average net assets	.67%	.83%	.82%	.77%	.79%	.80%	.73%	.78%	.78%	**.75%**
Portfolio turnover rate*	85%	126%	96%	96%	101%	87%	82%	135%	172%	**155%**
Shares outstanding at end of year (in thousands)	45,757	62,716	109,975	165,230	191,353	181,912	224,610	228,377	290,995	**363,632**

** In accordance with a Securities and Exchange Commission rules amendment, portfolio turnover rates after 1984 include U.S. government long-term securities that were excluded from the calculations in prior years.*

Table 6.3

Expenses and Performance

Expenses

Shareholder transaction expenses are charges you pay when you buy or sell shares of a fund.

Maximum sales charges on purchase (as a % of offering price)	3.00%
Maximum sales charge on reinvested dividends	None
Deferred sales charge on redemptions	None
Exchange fee	None

Annual fund operating expenses are paid out of the fund's assets. The fund pays management fees to FMR that vary based on the fund's performance. It also incurs other expenses for services such as maintaining shareholder records and furnishing shareholder statements and fund reports. The fund's expenses are factored into its share price or dividends and are not charged directly to shareholder accounts.

The following are projections based on historical expenses, and are calculated as a percentage of average net assets.

Management fee	.75%
12(b)-1 fee	None
Other expenses	.25%
Total fund operating expenses	1.00%

Example: Let's say, hypothetically, that the fund's annual return is 5 percent and that its operating expenses are exactly as just described. For every $1,000 you invested, here's how much you would have paid in total expenses if you closed your account after the number of years indicated:

After 1 year	$40
After 3 years	$61
After 5 years	$84
After 10 years	$149

This example illustrates the effect of expenses, but it is not meant to suggest actual or expected costs or returns, all of which may vary.

Understanding Expenses

Operating a mutual fund involves a variety of expenses for portfolio management, shareholder statements, tax reporting, and other services. As an investor, you pay some of these costs directly (for example, the fund's 3% sales charge). Others are paid from the fund's assets; the effect of these other expenses is already factored into any quoted share price or return.

you add up all the fund operating expenses, they amount to 1 percent of the fund's net assets.

So what does this mean to your bottom line? You can find that right below, which shows the cumulative impact of sales charges and expenses. If you invest $1,000 and earn 5 percent a year, you've spent $40 on sales and operating expenses in the first year; $61 after 3 years; and up to $149 after 10 years. Actually, a 5 percent assumed rate of return for this fund is absurd, and if that's all you thought you could earn, you certainly would not invest in it. However, that's not the point. The SEC requires funds to use such a reporting format account to make it easier for investors to compare fees and expenses.

If the fund is brand new, be sure to check whether the fund management company is subsidizing the fund's overhead or waiving management fees. Don't snub these funds—if someone's going to give you a free lunch, you might well want to take it. But free lunches don't last forever, and the relatively sumptuous returns subsidized funds can generate in their early years may not last when the fund company eventually cuts the subsidy.

Subsidies can also make a difference in how you perceive a fund. For instance, the prospectus for the Franklin U.S. Government Adjustable Rate Securities Fund reports that in the fiscal years ending January 31 of 1989, 1990, and 1991, the expense ratio was 0.44 percent, 0.39 percent, and 0.30 percent, respectively. Those are very good expense ratios for fixed-income funds. But the footnotes reveal that the fund manager was subsidizing fund expenses by waiving fees and paying some expenses out of its own pocket. Without the subsidies, the expense ratio would have been more than twice as much—0.96, 0.87, and 0.82 percent. Those ratios would make the fund unattractive to many pros.

The financial statements also give you some feeling for the fund. The numbers may look scary, but they're really pretty simple. Go to table 6.2. Start with the last column, which is for the fiscal year ending March 31, 1993. Investment income—income that was generated by dividends and interest paid by the fund's holdings—was $1.77 per share, not much considering the net asset value of $68 per share. But, like most growth funds, Magellan's mission is to provide capital appreciation, not current income. Still, as you can see in the next line, this investment income more than covered the fund's expenses of 57 cents per share, leaving net investment income of $1.20. The next line, "distributions from net investment income," indicates that the fund paid shareholders

dividends of $1.25 per share, a nickel more than they actually earned.

In a fund like Magellan, however, the big money is made from capital gains. Look at the line "net realized & unrealized gain (loss) on investments." When a mutual fund sells a security at a profit, it has a "realized" gain; when it sells at a loss, it's a realized loss. If a fund continues to hold stocks worth more than the fund paid for them, the stocks represent unrealized gains. Likewise, stocks valued at less than their cost are unrealized losses. To figure "net" gains, the fund tallies all gains and losses, including both realized and unrealized. If the number is positive, as it is here, the fund had net gains; if negative, net losses. In fiscal 1993, the Fidelity Magellan Fund had net gains of $9.18 per share.

Next, go down to the next line "distributions from net realized gain on investments." The figure for fiscal 1993 was $8.82 per share. That's what the fund paid in capital gains distributions to its shareholders during the year. As a percent of net gains, that's a relatively large number. In fiscal 1992, for instance, the fund had $9.21 in net gains but distributed only $5.43, and in fiscal 1991, the fund enjoyed net gains of $8.10 but distributed only $2.42. Why the difference in distributions? Mutual funds must distribute virtually all of their net realized gains. So if the distribution is high relative to net gains, as it was in fiscal 1993, that tells you the fund probably had a lot more realized than unrealized gains during the year. By the same analysis, in fiscal 1991, much of the gain was unrealized.

The next line, "net increase (decrease) in net asset value," shows 31 cents per share. Here's how that's computed: Remember the fund had net investment income of $1.20, but paid out $1.25. That takes 5 cents per share off the NAV. The fund also generated net gains of $9.18 but paid out $8.82, retaining 36 cents a share in NAV. Deduct the 5 cents from the 36, and you come up with 31 cents increase in NAV. Add that sum to the next figure, the $68.13 NAV at the beginning of the year, and you come up with $68.44—which was the NAV at the close of fiscal 1993.

The next group of figures, "ratios," helps you compare this fund to others. The ratio of net investment income to average net assets, 2.11 percent for the fiscal year, means little by itself. Compare it to the next line, "ratio of expenses to average net assets," which shows 1 percent. What these two numbers tell you is this: The fund generated net investment income amounting to 2.11 percent of assets, more than enough to pay the expenses of the fund, which ran 1 percent. (If a fund doesn't generate enough investment income to pay its own expenses, it pays them out of net gains or by selling assets.) That expense ratio includes the next line, "ratio of management fee to average net assets," which is 0.75 percent. Before moving on, look across at both the expense ratio and management fee lines—both trending downward. That's to be expected, since the Fidelity Magellan Fund is by far the largest equity fund and should have some economies of scale in its operations that benefit its shareholders. Be wary of funds in which the trends of these two ratios are moving up.

The last line, "portfolio turnover rate," 155 percent, means that during the year the fund bought and sold securities worth 1.55 times the total assets of the fund. If the fund owned $100 million in assets, it bought and sold $155 million worth of securities. In this case, the Fidelity Magellan Fund has nearly $25 billion in assets during this fiscal year, so it must have made securities trades worth more than $37.5 billion within twelve months.

Number of outstanding shares isn't particularly useful except for one thing—measuring the size of the fund. On March 31, the fund had 363,632,000 shares that were priced at $68.44 per share. Multiply the two figures and you get nearly $24.9 billion.

Investment Policy

After the financials, the prospectus turns to the investment objective, which will outline the overall strategy, the permitted investments in the broadest of terms (i.e., stocks or U.S. government or government-guaranteed securities), and restrictions, if any. Make sure the investment objective matches yours, and pay careful attention to how the fund managers plan to achieve it, especially the kinds of risk they might undertake (with *your* money).

Some fund managers try to boost yield by trading futures and options contracts. Others sacrifice net asset value in order to deliver a high payout. Is preservation of capital the utmost priority? Don't assume so, even if the investment is a government bond fund. Look for explicit statements in the prospectus, though they won't be couched in simple language.

The information in this section helps describe the fund's character. First Eagle Fund of America, for instance, says it will pursue capital appreciation with a flexible investment strategy that may include junk bonds, foreign securities, restricted securities (illiquid securities that are not publicly traded), and "special situations"—opportunities that may arise from liquidations, reorganizations, mergers, material litigation, technological breakthroughs, and new or currently existing management policies. Moreover, First Eagle makes clear that it may buy and sell options and futures contracts and even "leverage its assets for securities purchases"—that's another way to say the fund buys on margin.

Although not a mutual fund, the Orange County, California, general treasury got into trouble late in 1994 with this sort of strategy, and lost so much the county had to temporarily declare bankruptcy. Not all funds that borrow extra cash to sweeten their investment results run into problems, of course, but they can do so more easily than a fund that does not borrow.

If you'd sleep better with a fund that invests solely in well-known bluechips, without using margin, First Eagle is probably not for you.

Shareholder Services

Look for services and conveniences that should be described in the prospectus. Most money-market funds and many bond funds also offer checkwriting privileges, with a minimum check of $500 or $1,000. (United Services Treasury Securities Cash Fund is a U.S. money-market fund with no minimum check size, and no limit on the number of checks written.)

Automatic investing is an arrangement you set up between the fund company and your bank to make regular periodic transfers from your checking account to a designated mutual fund. It's an excellent way to accumulate capital, and, unlike a contractual arrangement that some funds still market, you can stop or alter the program at your discretion without penalty.

Most fund groups provide automatic reinvestment of dividends and capital gains distributions into new shares, a major benefit of investing in mutual funds since you can compound the growth rate of the fund by earning returns on your returns instead of taking these proceeds in cash.

Extra Loads Can Cut Into Profits

Although most load funds do not levy the load on reinvested shares, a few

still do, and this must be disclosed in the prospectus. If you plan to reinvest fund proceeds, you probably should shy away from funds with such charges. After all, while it's reasonable to compensate a sales rep for putting you into an investment, you may object to paying a commission on automatic reinvestments.

However, the load on reinvested dividends and capital gains may not be as onerous as some 12(b)-1 fees. Suppose you have $10,000 in a fund that paid out $500 this year, and you reinvest the proceeds, paying a 4 percent load. Your cost is 4 percent of $500, or $20. That $20 amounts to 0.2 percent of the entire $10,000 investment, far less that the 1 percent of the assets per year—in this case, $100—that the 12(b)-1 fees would amount to in many funds. What's more, funds that levy a 12(b)-1 fee do so whether or not shareholders are making money. The load on the reinvestment is charged only when there are profits to distribute.

Ultimately, your preference might depend on the total level of fees. For instance, consider Franklin's U.S. Government Securities Fund, which charges a 4 percent load on reinvestment. In one fiscal year, the fund paid 59.5 cents per share in distributions. A person with a $10,000 initial investment would have owned about 1333.333 shares (after paying the 4 percent load), generating income of $793. Reinvesting that income in the fund would have cost an additional $32 in sales charges. If the fund had a 0.50 percent 12(b)-1 charge instead of the load on reinvested dividends, the cost would have been about $51. If neither plan appeals to you, you're probably a candidate for no-load funds without 12(b)-1 fees.

Many funds allow you to redeem your earnings over the telephone.

Redemptions

Putting money into a mutual fund is simple. Fidelity Investments' walk-in centers, for instance, make investing easy by having personnel on hand to field questions, take applications, and accept checks. But though you can invest at one of these locations as if you were making a deposit at a local bank, you can't make an on-the-spot "withdrawal." The money must go through regular channels, either through a check by mail or a bank wire.

Getting money nevertheless can be almost as simple as putting it in if you do a little advance planning. Most funds offer telephone redemption privileges, but you won't get the money the day you make your first request. It's best to arrange for telephone redemptions when you initially open the account and set up transfers of your money to you by means of some fast, convenient way—check, wire transfer, or direct deposit in your account (available with Vanguard and some other fund families). If you want these services, the fund will ask for the appropriate banking information. Both the fund and your bank will usually charge for the service, and there may be a minimum amount that must be transferred.

Do the same with telephone switching privileges, so you're all set up to switch your funds instantaneously on the first day you want to. And don't assume that while some funds in a family of funds offer telephone redemption, all the others do.

Several of the Vanguard equity funds, for instance, are off-limits to telephone switches. There may even be limits on the amount of money you can withdraw or the number of switches you can order within a given period.

Plan on following the advice of a mutual fund timing service. Determine if the fund group has any limits on frequent switches. (That's something you may not find in the prospectus, so ask a fund representative.) Sometimes a fund group permits unlimited telephone switches between its equity, bond, and money-market funds but places restrictions on telephone withdrawals. On larger amounts, you may be asked to provide written instructions.

Obtaining quick access to your funds is especially important with money-market funds since you'll use them to hold liquid assets or "rainy day" emergency money. Set up all your money-fund accounts with check-writing and telephone redemption privileges. Even if you rarely use them, they can provide quick access to your assets when necessary.

Pay particular attention to all the fund's rules regarding withdrawals. Many funds need only a signature on a redemption letter. Others may specify that the signature be "guaranteed"—which requires an endorsement from a guarantor who compares the authenticity of the signature to one already on file and verifies that the signature is genuine. Some funds accept such guarantees from commercial banks, savings institutions, or brokerage firms that are members of the New York Stock Exchange. Ask the fund's service people to be sure.

One-Stop Shopping

If you opened a stock brokerage account and invested in, say, ten different stocks, you could keep track of them and trade them all through your one account. It's nearly impossible to do the same with mutual funds.

You can cut down on phone calls and mailings and make switches between funds a lot simpler by investing with one fund family. The downside is that it's so limiting. Although you would gain in convenience, you would have less variety of funds to choose from.

When you're buying load funds through a broker or financial planner, the professional is a doorway to the mutual fund world. But be aware that such an arrangement restricts you to the load funds with which your advisor has sales agreements.

Other planners offer access to a greater number of funds by managing portfolios of no-load funds. They usually charge an annual management fee, perhaps 1 percent, based on the amount of assets under management. (This management fee is over and

Table 6.4

Fund Shopping Through Discount Brokers

	Toll-free Phone	Local Phone
K. Aufhauser & Company	800-368-3668	
Barry Murphy & Company	800-221-2111	
Charles Schwab & Company	800-435-4000	
Seaport Securities	800-221-9894	212-482-8689
Waterhouse Securities	800-934-4443	
Jack White & Company	800-233-3411	619-587-2000

A discount brokerage can make investing more accessible by offering low- and no-fee funds.

above whatever fees the fund companies charge.)

The discount brokerage firm of Charles Schwab & Company runs a program called Mutual Fund Marketplace (see table 6.4) that offers one-stop access to about 700 funds, most of them no-load. Within these 700 funds, investors can buy at least 200 with no-load and no fee. Schwab is paid for its services by the fund companies, often through a 12(b)-1 charge. For the other no-load funds, you pay the broker directly: 0.6 percent of the investment on trades up to $15,000, 0.2 percent on the next $85,000, and 0.08 percent on everything over $100,000. Schwab officials say that, on average, clients in the Mutual Fund Marketplace program end up paying commissions of about 0.3 percent of the amount invested.

So why pay Schwab to invest in a fund that doesn't charge commissions? If all you ever plan to do is buy one fund, there is no valid reason. Similarly, if you're stashing away a couple hundred dollars a month in a fund, Schwab's minimum commission makes it cheaper to deal directly with that fund. But if you buy many funds and make large transactions, you may value the convenience of a consolidated statement for all your mutual fund investments, with one Form 1099 at tax time. Furthermore, if you sell one fund and redistribute the proceeds into three other funds, it's far easier to do it within your Schwab account than by switching money among many different ones.

Another advantage is that there are some excellent funds with high minimum investments. For example, two PIMCO bond funds, Low Duration and Total Return, ask for $500,000 minimums, but through Schwab you can buy in for as little as $1,000. Schwab lowers these thresholds because it maintains an "omnibus" account with each no-load fund, pooling the money from many different clients. PIMCO treats all Schwab customers as one account, while Schwab keeps track of how many shares of that account belong to each customer.

Schwab has even extended the Mutual Fund Marketplace program to load funds like American, Colonial, Franklin, Pioneer, Putnam, and Templeton, too, although regulations bar brokers from discounting these loads. Still, buying a load fund through a discount broker may appeal to investors who want to own the funds without enduring the pestering from full-service brokers who want more business from them.

Fidelity Investments' FundsNetwork program is similar to Schwab's, offering 1,500 no-load and load funds, 200 of them without a transaction fee. For transactions up to $5,000, the fee is $17.50 plus 0.8 percent of the principal, with a $28 minimum. On a $3,000 purchase, that works out to $41.50.

Other discount brokers run broad-based mutual fund programs similar to Schwab's. Jack White & Company offers about 900 no-load and low-load funds. The minimum charge is $27 per trade on trades of up to $5,000, $35 for trades of $5,001 to $25,000, and $50 for trades in excess of $50,000. Jack White also has a no-fee service arrangement with about 285 funds. Load-fund investors may also check out Jack White's CONNECT System, which allows investors to buy load funds for a flat $200 fee, no matter how large the purchase. By comparison, if you place $25,000 in a fund with a 6 percent front-end load, you'd pay $1,500 off the top.

The CONNECT System works by placing a buyer's offer on an electronic bulletin board and looking for a seller. CONNECT pays half the fee, or $100, to the seller as an incentive to sell through the Jack White system instead of cashing out directly through the fund company. CONNECT doesn't guarantee that it can always match buyers and sellers, but the system is expected to become part of a securities dealer's electronic bulletin board, which will enable Jack White to attract fund buyers and sellers.

The convenience and simplicity of such programs are making them increasingly popular with mutual fund "market-timers," investors who move assets around, following rigorous technical formulas, trying to capture upside moves in the stock market while steering clear of downdrafts.

Buying on Margin

For more aggressive investors, the Schwab program (and perhaps a few others) allows the purchase of mutual funds on "margin." Margin buying is simply borrowing. It works this way:

Suppose you think small company stocks are about to stage a big rally and decide to invest $10,000 in the Twentieth Century Ultra Fund. If the fund goes up 20 percent in the next six months, your investment is worth $12,000 and you can take a profit of $2,000. However, if you buy on margin, you can own $20,000 worth of shares in the fund—$10,000 of your own money and $10,000 loaned from the brokerage firm using your original investment as collateral. The interest rate on the loan is usually the broker's loan rate (a figure similar to a bank's prime rate) plus anywhere from 0.5 to 1.5 percent, depending on the loan size.

If the fund goes up 20 percent, your holding climbs to $24,000, and if you sell it, you've earned a $4,000 profit on your original $10,000 investment—a 40 percent return. However, you took a loan from the broker to buy the shares, so you owe interest. Ten thousand dollars borrowed for six months at 8 percent interest comes out to $400. All told, you net (before commissions) $3,600 on your original $10,000, compared to only $2,000 without margin.

Not all margin plays work out so well as the above scenario. If the value of the investment remained unchanged for six months, you're still out the interest. Worse yet, if the fund declined by 20 percent, your $20,000 investment is now worth $16,000 (but you still owe $10,000 on it). If you sell at that point, you repay the broker the $10,000 originally borrowed plus the $400 interest to boot, leaving you with only $5,400 out of your initial $10,000 investment.

What's more, when the investment is worth $16,000, the broker will no longer lend you the full $10,000. Fifty percent is the usual percentage allowed. You'll have to come up with another $2,000 in cash, or the broker will sell all or part of your investment without your permission and take back the money you owe.

Clearly, you shouldn't use margin buying unless you know *exactly* what you're doing and can withstand the potential loss.

Chapter 7

Building an Investment Portfolio

You've been reading about some of the new wonder drugs on the market, and you give your doctor a call: "Doc, these new drugs sound great. How about writing me some prescriptions for the two or three that you think are best?" Sounds absurd, doesn't it?

Yet many investors choose their investments the same way. They hear about a hot-performing fund or a fund with a novel investment twist, and jump in. Instead, they should examine their financial goals and decide what they want to achieve (see table 7.1). Only then can they make sensible choices from the multitude of investment opportunities. There are hundreds of excellent mutual funds, but not every one is appropriate for every investor.

Determining Your Financial Goals

The 35-year-old physician with two preschool-aged children needs to build capital—and has time on her side. She

would probably benefit from a fairly aggressive mix of funds, dividing her investments equally among maximum-growth funds, less aggressive-growth funds, small-company funds, and international funds.

The 45-year-old computer programmer, having built some savings through aggressive investing, may settle for a lower return to reduce the risk in his investment portfolio. Facing years of college tuition payments for his children, he wants to be sure the money will remain available. So he's keeping at least one year's worth of tuition payments in a short-term bond fund like the Neuberger/Berman Limited Maturity Bond Fund and has put the proceeds from some of his growth funds into less volatile growth-and-income portfolios like AIM Charter. He has cut his maximum-growth, international stock, and small-company funds holdings down to about 60 percent of his portfolio, instead of the 75 percent more appropriate in earlier years.

The 55-year-old lawyer is finished with his children's education and is now socking away his money for anticipated retirement in about 10 years. His single biggest allocation is 25 percent to growth-and-income funds like FPA Perennial. He has no maximum-growth funds, but he does have growth, international, and small-company holdings.

His friend, also age 55, a corporate executive worried about downsizing and early retirement, is lowering his portfolio's exposure to risk by moving assets from aggressive equity funds to growth-and-income funds, as well as to equity-income funds, like Invesco Industrial Income. He chooses intermediate-term bond funds like Benham GNMA Income for the fixed-income portion of his portfolio.

Mutual funds, like all investments, are only a means to an end. Use them to accumulate a down payment for a home, college tuition money for your children, or a nest egg for your retirement. Before you choose any particular mutual funds, however, you must know the goal you're trying to achieve.

The conventional wisdom says you should be willing to accept more

Table 7.1

Before Investing, Consider . . .

- Do you need current income from your investments?
- How soon will you need the proceeds of your investments?
- How will inflation affect you?
- How much risk are you willing to take?
- How will taxes affect your investments?
- What kind of temperment do you have for investing?

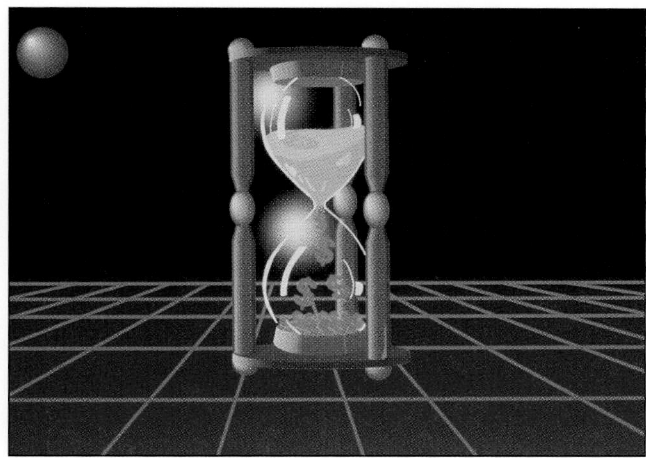

Determine whether you can afford to invest short- or long-term before you make an investment.

risk when you're younger and then gradually shift to safer investments as you near and enter retirement. But this is only a general rule. There's plenty of flexibility for you to satisfy your individual needs and preferences. To help choose the most appropriate funds for your investment program, answer the following series of questions:

Do You Need Current Income from Your Investments?

If you regularly spend the income from your certificates of deposit and the dividends from your stock holdings, you obviously need current income. Most people interested in current income are retirees, but younger families and single parents may also want this extra cash for spending.

To determine how much current income you need from your investments, start by estimating your total annual needs. Then subtract salaries, pensions, and all other sources. Your investment target will be to meet or exceed the remaining, uncovered portion of your financial needs. Suppose Investment A yields about 7.5 percent and Investment B yields about 4 percent. Based on this scenario, in order to earn $10,000 in extra income from your investments you'll need to place about $135,000 in Invest A, or about $250,000 in Invest B. If you have more money than this, of course, you can invest the extra for capital appreciation, against the day when $10,000 per year won't be adequate.

If you can meet all your income needs without tapping investment income, you'd probably be wise to invest for growth—but vary your strategy according to the economic times and opportunities. For example, when interest rates are high, money-market funds become very attractive because of their safety and the large amounts of interest they pay. When rates are low, stocks and bonds often do better.

How Soon Will You Need the Proceeds of Your Investments?

Identifying the right time horizon helps you find the right funds. If your goal is 15 years away—say, to pay college tuition for your preschooler—you can rely primarily on equity funds. Over long periods of time they generally outperform bond and money-market funds. If your goal is closer than 10 years, you'll want to put more of your assets into short- and intermediate-term fixed-income funds. Cash you'll need in a year or less should go into a money-market fund.

Some people argue that "long-term" is just a series of "short-terms," back to back, but there are major differences in the returns you can generate in investments geared to different time horizons.

Over more than 60 years, U.S. Treasury bills have paid about 3.7 percent, on average, and long-term government bonds have paid about 4.8 percent. The comparable return on common stocks has been 10.3 percent per year! Over a more recent 30-year period, T-bills and bonds have paid about 6.3 percent, but stocks still paid about 10.3 percent. Putting your investments into a short-term investment when you had a long-term time horizon would in this case have been an expensive mistake!

How Will Inflation Affect You?

You'll eventually use your investment dollars to purchase goods and services. That's why inflation—the erosion of purchasing power—is a critical factor in planning your portfolio.

Think of it this way: You invest $1,000 in a 30-year bond paying 6.2 percent interest. Twice a year you collect $31, and after 30 years you get back your original $1,000. Today, that $31 buys dinner in a moderate restaurant. But what will it buy in the future? If inflation averages only 3 percent, your $31 will be worth only $23 a decade from now; at 6 percent inflation, only $17. Ten years from now, that $31 may buy only lunch for one, instead of dinner for two. And the process continues for 20 more years. The same happens with your principal. At 3 percent annual inflation, after 30 years your $1,000 has the purchasing power of only $412.

To inflation-proof your mutual fund portfolio, buy equity funds, especially small-company funds. Over the long haul, these beat the Consumer Price Index hands down. True, there are times—as in the 1970s—when inflation outpaces the stock market, but small-company stocks have consistently stood their ground even during inflationary periods.

Another way to guard against inflation is to buy international stock and bond funds. Since inflation tends to erode the value of the dollar, assets denominated in foreign currencies go up, providing you with a hedge against the declining value of your dollars.

How Much Risk Are You Willing to Take?

"No pain, no gain" is a common phrase these days, and it applies to

Consider the risks, such as inflation, when deciding how much you are able to invest.

Take only the risks you can afford.

investments as well as anything else. For investments, however, pain is better understood as *risk* and *volatility*.

Many investors are so averse to risk that they stop making objective judgments. Psychologists tell us that most of us shy away from risks in our financial decisions, probably because we're more influenced by the fear of loss than by the prospect of gain. In fact, some studies show that the pain of loss is twice as large as the pleasure of an equivalent gain.

If you're like most investors, you have probably erred on the side of caution. You've underestimated the amount of risk you can absorb and are now paying for this dearly in terms of lost opportunities. For proof, notice what happens when companies give employees the option of directing their own pension funds. These employees overwhelmingly choose fixed-income investments, compared with professional investment managers, who generally favor more lucrative but riskier stocks over bonds.

Your ability to absorb risks is greatly increased when you have a long time horizon. Here's why: Although stocks average about a 10.3 percent average annual return, fluctuation does occur from year to year. Although any one year can bring you losses, the longer you hold stocks, the closer your gains will approach the 10.3 percent annual average.

How Will Taxes Affect Your Investments?

Most investment advisers caution you against investing solely to save on taxes. The best investments are those that make sound economic sense, with tax benefits only a secondary consideration.

Once you've identified a good investment, you should see how it influences your ultimate tax bill. To do this, you must know the tax rate imposed on your next dollar of income. To minimize taxes, concentrate your assets in growth and maximum-growth funds. Generally, these funds pay few if any dividends, so you'll escape current taxes there. They also tend to hold stocks for longer periods, reducing the percentage of profits that become taxable during the year.

If you want to put money in fixed-income or money-market funds, consider the federal and/or state tax-free ones available to you. Many times their yields are comparable to the after-tax yields of conventional, taxable funds.

Don't let yourself get overwhelmed by investments. If you are a novice, take on investments that you are comfortable with and buy more later.

The best way to defer taxes may be to invest within an Individual Retirement Account (IRA), a Keogh plan, or some other tax-deferring program. You'll pay no taxes on gains from any source until you begin withdrawals, years from now.

What Kind of Temperament for Investing Do You Have?

It's one thing to coolly and rationally consider income needs, time horizons, taxes, and the like, and come up with objective conclusions about where to invest your money. But if you shudder at the thought of losing principal, or worry about every twist and turn of the stock market, or become "stressed out" if your investment loses value—even for a little while—you should factor these emotional concerns into your investment plans. Don't be ashamed to move cautiously. Advice comes from others, but the money that's invested on that advice comes from *you.*

In her work on the psychological characteristics of individual investors, Marilyn MacGruder Barnewall, a financial consultant, has described both a "passive" and an "active" investor. Passive investors—and that's most of us, including professional investment managers—have a greater need for security than tolerance for risk. In fact, we usually perceive risks to be greater than they actually are. Passive investors are more likely to use brokers and investment advisers or professional services, and to buy broker-sold funds. Active investors, in contrast, have generally earned their wealth in their lifetimes. These people understand how to take risks and have a higher tolerance for risk than a need for security. In fact, they often underestimate the risks they take. Since they usually feel more comfortable with investments they control, active investors take less advice from brokers and other advisors or investment professionals and make investment decisions more on their own. Of course, most people actually show a combination of characteristics from both of these descriptions.

The investment counseling firm of Bailard Biehl & Kaiser has identified four investor profiles: Adventurers, Celebrities, Individuals, and Guardians. Adventurers like risk and often make intuitive judgments. Celebrities follow investment fashion, preferring to do what's hot rather than what's best. Individuals are entrepreneurial, and take a methodical, rational approach to investing. Guardians are concerned about preserving their wealth and eagerly seek guidance to do so.

You may spot some of your own traits in these descriptions. If you're too adventurous or too much of a celebrity, consider restraining these traits somewhat in favor of your individualist traits, which often produce better investment results.

Putting It All Together

By this time, you know what you want from your investments and have a good idea of what kind of investor you are. But you still need to choose one or more mutual funds, and actually transfer your money.

With so many potentially lucrative ones available, you can easily become overwhelmed. To avoid this, think about the categories of funds (as described in chapters 2–5), and in what proportions you want to own them. Stay alert to the marketplace, because fund managers also develop new funds to pursue new investment opportunities.

Next, put enough cash to live for six months, or longer, into a money-market fund (taxable or tax-free). If you ever tap into it, be sure to replenish it later.

Your Asset Allocation Plan

Your asset allocation plan is essentially a strategy for effectively dividing up your assets. For example, you may decide to allocate your portfolio 50 percent into U.S. equities, 30 percent into bonds, 10 percent into foreign stocks, and 10 percent into foreign bonds. Or you may decide on an entirely different arrangement, and may change it from year to year.

Money managers devise asset allocation plans using elaborate computer models, but some popular personal finance software, such as Andrew Tobias's Managing Your Money, can also help you develop a good plan. Software is particularly useful in showing the relative overall risk of different asset allocation plans.

If you're working with a broker or financial planner, he or she can help you develop an asset allocation plan. Even mutual fund companies are helping investors with asset allocation. Fidelity Investments, for example, offers FundMatch, a package of workbooks, toll-free telephone advice, consultations, seminars, and software. Dreyfus Corporation asks investors to

Take the time to sit down and review your portfolio, and determine if your money is where you want it to be.

Mutual Funds Risk Spectrum

Are specialized funds riskier than diversified equity funds? How much risk is there in bond funds compared to equity funds? Here's a chart that can help investors understand the relative risk of various types of mutual funds. The risk scale goes from 0 to 7, with 0 defined as no risk. Money-market funds are not on the chart, since there are no fluctuations in their net asset value (NAV). Some specialized funds, like technology and precious metals, are at the high end of the risk spectrum. The NAVs of these funds can fluctuate sharply.

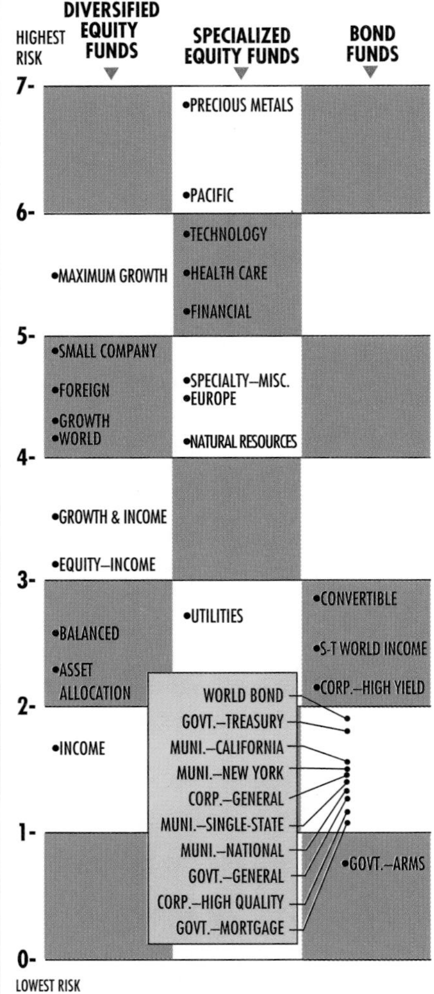

fill out a questionnaire and gives them a sample asset allocation plan based on their answers.

There are nearly an infinite variety of asset allocation plans possible. Don't accept the first one that crosses your desk. Instead, tinker with the percentages, the categories, and the risk factors until the plan feels right for you.

Once you have an asset allocation plan you feel comfortable with, mutual funds provide an easy way to implement it. The various categories of funds, and individual funds within categories, allow you to fine-tune the allocation of your assets.

If you're not motivated to create your own asset allocation plan, consider the "fund of funds" approach. T. Rowe Price, for example, offers funds that invest in a spectrum of other Price funds, or you could select a balanced fund, like American, Fidelity, or Phoenix, which builds portfolios containing both equities and bonds.

Look to Your Time Horizon

Since stocks are consistently the best long-term investments, mutual fund investors with long time horizons should allocate a significant portion of their portfolios to equity funds.

If your time horizon is between 10 and 20 years—this is appropriate for most 40- and 50-year-olds—you might begin lowering your risk by moving some of your assets into more conservative equity and bond funds. Even at retirement, however, your time horizon is long enough for equity funds to have a place in your portfolio.

Based on age group, here are five different portfolio mixes you might want to evaluate and consider:

For Your 20s: Go for growth-oriented funds, but keep some assets in low-risk, short-term bonds funds. *Asset allocation:* 20 percent growth or maximum-growth; 20 percent small-company; 20 percent international stock; 40 percent money-market or short-term funds.

For Your 30s: Go for long-term growth to pay for college or other family expenses in coming years. *Asset allocation:* 25 percent maximum-growth; 25 percent small-company;

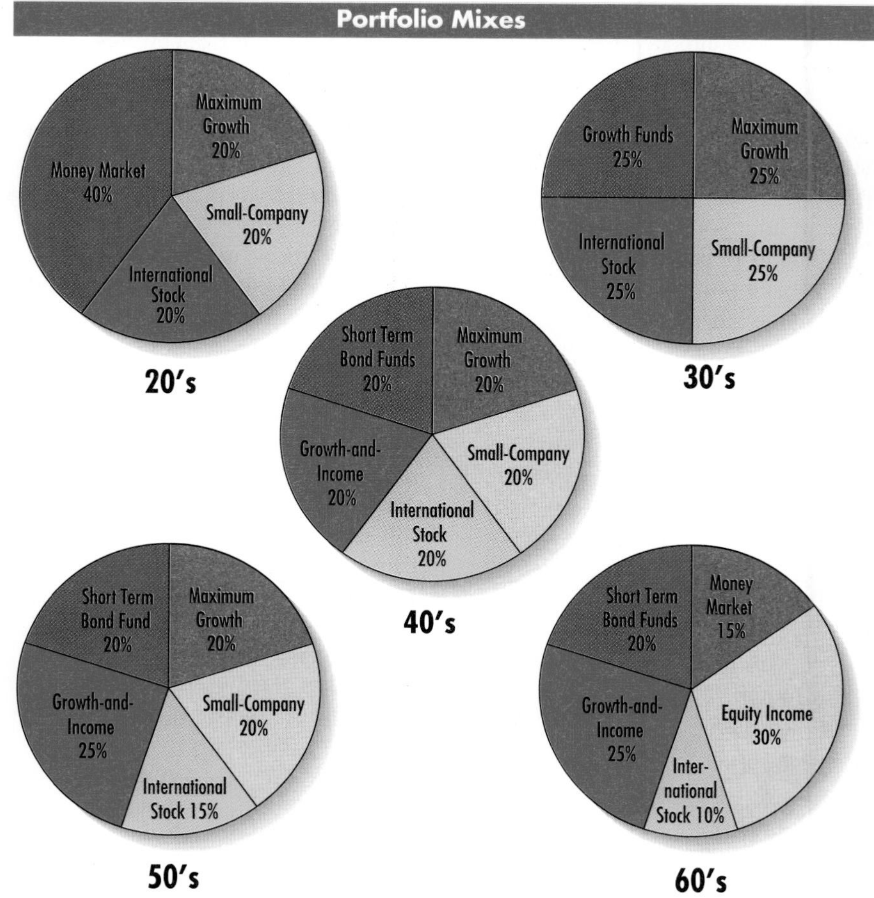

25 percent international stock; 25 percent growth funds.

For Your 40s: With growing financial security, turn a bit more cautious. Lower your overall portfolio risk but still keep some assets in long-term growth vehicles. *Asset allocation:* 20 percent maximum-growth; 20 percent small-company; 20 percent international stock; 20 percent growth-and-income; 20 percent short- or intermediate-term bond funds.

For Your 50s: With children leaving the nest, your income requirements may be smaller. Save more, and invest for retirement. *Asset allocation:* 20 percent growth; 20 percent small-company; 15 percent international stock; 25 percent growth-and-income; 20 percent short- or intermediate-term bond funds.

For Your 60s: Nearing or in retirement, you have many years of life and experiences ahead of you. Plan for it by continuing to grow your capital—with safety. *Asset allocation:* 15 percent money market; 30 percent equity-income; 10 percent international stock; 25 percent growth-and-income; 20 percent short- or intermediate-term bond funds.

Diversification

Suppose you've decided to allocate your assets among growth, maximum-growth, small-company, and international funds. How many different funds should you buy in each of the categories? One good rule of thumb is to put no more than 20 percent of your total portfolio into any one fund or fund family. Thus, if you're putting more than this amount into a given category, you'll need to select two or more good funds within it. If your portfolio is very extensive, you might want to limit your investment in any one fund to 10 percent, or even 5 percent of your portfolio.

On the other hand, investing in too many different funds will burden you with extra paperwork, and since most mutual funds practice diversification within their own investments, you gain little from buying too many funds. If you're buying load funds (those with a sales charge), spreading your portfolio too thin may prevent you from qualifying for any quantity discounts that are available.

Making Your First Investment

Once you've clarified your investment objectives and selected some funds, your next step is to make the actual investments. From this point, don't hesitate to take action, because you may be missing important economic action that works to your benefit.

If you're having trouble taking the first step into mutual funds, consider a gradual conversion of your portfolio to mutual funds. For example, if you have $25,000 to invest, make individual $5,000 investments at intervals during the next year. Keep the rest of your portfolio where it is, or put it into money-market funds. You'll make your next $5,000 investment in three months, and again three months after that, and so on, until you're fully invested. This way, you'll take advantage of a rising market, but you'll have a chance to buy in at a lower price if the market temporarily goes against you.

One common mistake is to "wait for the next buying opportunity," when the market or interest rates reach a top or a bottom. After all, if you could reliably find the tops and bottoms, you'd already be playing the futures or options markets and making a bundle.

The precise moment that you plunk down your money can certainly make a difference, but probably not because your hunch about a market top or a bottom is correct. If you're considering a taxable fund, for example, don't buy just before a dividend or capital gains distribution. You can learn these dates by calling the fund's toll-free customer service line. Because these funds must distribute to investors nearly all their income and realized capital gains, by law, the share price fluctuates—often predictably—just after a distribution.

Here's a hypothetical example: Suppose you invest $10,000 in a mutual fund and get 1,000 shares. The fund managers then pay out a dividend of $1 per share. Your shares will drop by the same $1, so your 1,000 shares will be worth $9,000, but you'll have the $1,000 dividend, so you haven't lost. Not yet. The problem is, you'll owe tax on that distribution as though it were income, even though it hasn't increased the value of your holdings. So buying just before a distribution has the effect of converting some of your original principal into income—taxable income!

It's far better, therefore, to invest just after a dividend, or at least well before the next one, so your money has a chance to actually earn some of the income on which you'll be taxed.

Now let's examine the impact of trying to time your investments in mutual funds. *Business Week* asked Morningstar, Inc., which provides highly regarded data on mutual fund performance, to measure the total return generated by 727 equity funds between August 25, 1987 (when the

Dow was at a high-water mark of 2722) and September 1, 1988 (when the Dow closed at 2752). During that period, the market had gone through a rollercoaster 1,000 point decline and recovery.

The mutual funds, for the most part, did an admirable job for their shareholders—even those who, in retrospect, invested on the worst day of the year. Approximately 80 percent of the funds did better than break even, and about 56 percent of the funds, more than 400 of them, beat the 9 percent return earned by the Dow 30 industrial stocks during that period. More than 40 percent, about 300 funds, beat the 13 percent total return chalked up by the Standard & Poor's 500 Stock Index during the period. The average U.S. diversified equity fund returned 11 percent. All funds averaged 9.6 percent, slightly above the return on the Dow.

Here's another measure of the impact of time. The T. Rowe Price mutual fund group calculated the returns earned by two imaginary investors. Both invest $2,000 in the stock market once each year over 20 years, for a total of $40,000. One invests on the day the market reaches its lowest point for the year, the other on the day the market hits its high for the year. Between 1969 and 1989, the perfect market-timer would have finished with a portfolio worth $226,365, a 13.5 percent average annual return, while his bad-luck companion would nevertheless have earned a whopping $175,422, for an 11.4 percent average annual return. There's probably not as much of a difference between them as you would have expected, and, as a practical matter, most investors' results would fall somewhere in the middle.

Bond funds are thought to be very safe, but they also fluctuate. When rates begin to drop, most investors who like fixed-income vehicles try to buy, if only to lock in the higher yields before they disappear. But when rates fall, bond prices rise. So investors chasing yields are buying into a rising market.

It may not be necessary to chase intermediate- and long-term bonds. Odds are you'll see today's prices and yields again in a few years. In a recent six-year period, for example, the rate on long-term U.S. government bonds fluctuated between 5.8 percent and 10.2 percent. In contrast to stock prices, which can theoretically rise forever, bond prices are constrained by these interest rate fluctuations. If rates go to 5 percent, today's bond prices will look cheap. But that would require inflation of only half a percent—highly unlikely. Over time, bond prices vary, but only within a trading range. So if you miss the bond price you want, don't worry. Just wait a bit, and you'll probably see it again.

Dollar-Cost Averaging

When you invest regularly in mutual funds over a long time period, as in a 401(k) or other savings-incentive plan, you're engaged in a time-honored practice called "dollar-cost averaging." This simply means you're investing a constant amount of dollars at regular intervals. When the price of the investment is low, your dollars buy more of it; when prices are high, your dollars buy less. But so long as the investment's total return is generally rising, dollar-cost averaging almost ensures that your average cost is less than the current price. It also guarantees you the lowest average price over the period.

Let's look at this a little closer by examining table 7.2. Imagine you're electronically moving $200 per month from your checking account into an equity mutual fund—for example, Twentieth Century Ultra Investors. If you started in January 1990, your price per share would have been $8.62, so

Table 7.2

How Dollar-Cost Averaging Works for Fund Investors

In January 1990, an investor decided to start a program of dollar-cost averaging. He selected Twentieth Century Ultra Investors, and decided to invest $200 on the first business day of every month, and reinvest any dividends or capital gains if and when they're paid.

1990 Summary: Invested $2,407.96, purchased 285.166 shares at an average cost of $8.44 per share

Date	Price/share	Shares purchased	Total shares
January	$8.62	23.202	23.2020
February	7.66	26.110	49.3120
March	7.91	25.284	74.5960
April	8.15	24.540	99.1360
May	8.11	24.661	123.797
June	9.38	21.322	145.119
July	9.48	21.097	166.216
August	9.18	21.786	188.002
September	8.51	23.502	211.504
October	8.18	24.450	235.954
November	7.76	25.773	261.727
December	8.86	22.573	284.300
Dec. 29 paid capital gains distribution of 0.028 per share, or $7.96			
	9.19	0.866	285.166

1991 Summary: Invested $2,400.00, purchased 187.184 shares at an average cost of $12.82 per share

Date	Price/share	Shares purchased	Total shares
January	$9.12	21.930	307.096
February	10.86	18.416	329.026
March	11.71	17.079	346.105
April	12.97	15.420	361.525
May	12.63	15.835	377.360
June	13.48	14.837	392.197
July	12.64	15.823	408.020
August	13.87	14.420	422.220
September	14.51	13.784	436.004
October	14.69	13.615	449.619
November	15.42	12.970	462.589
December	15.32	13.055	475.644

No capital gains distribution

1992 Summary: Invested $2,400.00, purchased 152.164 shares at an average cost of $15.77 per share

Date	Price/share	Shares purchased	Total shares
January	$17.34	11.534	487.178
February	17.61	11.357	498.712
March	17.39	11.501	510.213
April	16.19	12.353	522.566
May	14.93	13.396	535.962
June	15.50	12.903	548.865
July	14.58	13.717	562.582
August	15.27	13.098	575.680
September	14.55	13.746	589.426
October	14.59	13.708	603.134
November	15.56	12.853	615.987
December	16.67	11.998	627.985

No capital gains distribution

1993 Summary: Invested $2,400.00, purchased 124.837 shares at an average cost of $19.23 per share

Date	Price/share	Shares purchased	Total shares
January	$17.29	11.567	639.552
February	18.30	10.929	650.481
March	16.55	12.085	662.566
April	17.36	11.521	674.087
May	17.53	11.409	685.496
June	19.43	10.293	695.789
July	19.93	10.035	705.824
August	20.11	9.945	715.769
September	21.45	9.324	725.093
October	21.99	9.095	734.188
November	21.89	9.137	743.325
December	21.06	9.497	752.822

No capital gains distribution

After four years the investor has invested $9,600 out of his pocket, plus another $7.96 from investment of distributions. He owns 752.822 shares at an average cost of $12.76 per share. On Dec. 31, 1993, the price per share is $21.39. The total investment is worth $16,102.86.

your first month's investment would have purchased 23.202 shares. In February, the price dropped to $7.66, so the $200 would purchase 26.11 shares. By July, the price was up to $9.48. Now the $200 would buy only about 21 shares.

By early December, you would have accumulated 284.3 shares, when the fund's capital gains distribution of $0.28 per share brought you enough to buy another 0.86 shares. During the year, you acquired 285.16 shares at an average cost of $8.44 each.

After four years, your total $9,600 investment would have netted you 752.822 shares at an average cost of $12.76. However, those shares were then selling at $21.39, making your investment worth almost $16,103!

Switch Funds! The Timing Game

While mutual funds are generally presented as long-term investments, the advent of fund families containing many different investment strategies, and low- or no-cost switching privileges for investors, has given rise to a new mutual fund strategy: timing the market and rapidly switching funds to take advantage of current trends.

The idea is similar to buying and selling stocks, except that your money nearly always stays within a single mutual fund family, and there's far less commission cost for each trade. The key to success in this strategy is accurate "market-timing," that is, to

Table 7.3

The Market-Timing Game

Newsletter	Timing System	Average Annual Total Return*
Systems & Forecasts	Time Trend-Cash on Sales	17.1%
Market Logic	Seasonality Trading Plan	15.4
Market Logic	Recommended Market Exposure	13.7
Telephone Switch Newsletter	Equity/Cash Timing Model	13.4
Value Line Investment	Survey Market Timing Model	13.2
Professional Timing Service	Supply/Demand Formula	13.1
Big Picture	Short-Term Trading Guide (SGA)	12.9
Elliott Wave Theorist	Investors-Cash on Sales	12.5
Outlook	Market Allocations	12.0
Dines Letter	Short-Term Signals	11.2
Granville Market Letter	Cash on Sales	11.1
Fund Exchange	Fund Timing Model	11.0
Dow Theory Letters	Grading of Primary Trend	11.0
Bob Nurock's Advisory	Technical Market Index-Cash on Sales	10.5
Professional Tape Reader	Mutual Fund Portfolio	8.4
Benchmarks		
Standard & Poor's 500 (with dividends)		14.9%
Wilshire 5000 Value Weighted Total Return Index		14.2
U.S. Diversified Equity Funds		13.1
U.S. Treasury Bill Portfolio		6.4

*Jan. 1, 1984–Dec. 31, 1993

invest early in the market's upswings and to sell before much of the subsequent downturns occur. No-load equity funds seem tailor-made for market-timing, since they cost nothing to buy or sell, and they contain a diversified basket of stocks.

The idea of market-timing is very appealing, and many newsletters and other advisers have become very successful by selling "timing" advice (see table 7.3). Nevertheless, given the facts we've revealed in our discussion of the relative success of investors who bought at the tops and bottoms of the market over a 20-year period, there's still room for skepticism about the true value of market-timing.

One of the biggest problems with market-timing is that the stock market makes most of its gains in relatively short periods. Throughout the 1980s, for example, the S&P 500 returned 17.6 percent per year. But if you take out the ten days when stocks made their largest gains, the average return for the decade drops to 12.6 percent! Take out the 20 most profitable days and the average return further falls to 9.3 percent!

Market-timers who are unlucky enough to miss the few important days severely hamper their chances for success. Unless you know for sure when the market will make its big gains, buy-and-hold seems a better strategy.

The profits from market-timing are further reduced when you trade with taxable mutual funds, since your net profits immediately become subject to income tax.

Chapter 8

Monitoring Your Mutual Funds

Now that you have a portfolio of mutual funds, you may be tempted to leave your mutual funds on autopilot and just watch your fortune mount up. This is unadvisable. While many mutual funds are buy-and-hold investments, none is buy-and-forget!

Tracking Funds in the Financial Pages

Mutual fund prices are quoted daily in *The Wall Street Journal*, *Investors Business Daily*, and just about any newspaper that carries daily financial tables. In addition, Sunday newspapers usually have mutual fund tables that indicate the high, low, and last prices for the week.

Not every fund makes it into the newspapers, though. To qualify, the fund needs a minimum of 1,000 shareholders or $25 million in assets. Until recently, most newspapers carried the same mutual fund tables, containing several columns of fund prices in dollars and cents, with funds presented alphabetically first by family and then by fund name.

These traditional tables show the fund's net asset value, followed by the offer price, which is the NAV plus any front-end load, and finally the daily price change, which usually amounts to pennies per day for most mutual funds.

In addition, there are letters that serve to footnote such features as 12(b)-1 plans, redemption fees, and income or capital gains distributions. More than 600 newspapers still carry this basic table, distributed by the Associated Press.

Some newspapers are starting to offer more—and potentially more confusing—information. *The Wall Street Journal,* for instance, now supplements the NAV, offer price, and NAV change with the fund's investment objective and year-to-date return, plus several columns of data that fluctuate from day to day. The *Journal*'s data come from Lipper Analytical Services, Inc. Check your favorite newspaper for details of what's listed, and when.

If you're familiar with stock tables, you'll notice that mutual fund pricing goes to the penny—$8.71, or $15.46, or $65.03, or whatever, compared with stock price quotes typically given in quarters, eighths, or even sixteenths of a dollar. The daily movement of mutual funds seems almost glacial compared to stocks.

One reason is that mutual funds are highly diversified pools of securities that frequently move in opposite directions at the same time, canceling out big moves. For example, if there are 100 stocks in a fund, 50 may have gone up, 40 may have gone down, and 10 may not have changed. Unless the market moves dramatically, the mutual funds drift very slowly from day to day.

Dreyfus:		
A Bond	13.46	+.02
Aprec p	15.36	+.05
AssetAll	12.60	+.04
Balncd	13.69	+.03
BasicMu	12.33	+.03
CalInt	12.71	+.03
CT Int	12.71	+.04
CorVInst	24.80	+.02
CorVIv p	24.80	+.02
DiscpR	17.50	+.07
Dreyf	12.16	...
EdEllnd	12.07	+.12
FL Int	12.75	+.03
GNM p	14.04	+.02
GMBd p	14.08	+.06
GrInc	15.78	–.02
GthOp	8.22	–.01
InsMu p	16.87	+.07
Interm	13.38	+.03
InterEq p	13.28	–.09
InvGN	14.32	+.01
MA Int	12.42	+.04
MunBd	11.92	+.05
NJ Int	12.79	+.04
NwLd r	31.01	–.04
NYIn p	10.89	+.03
NYTE p	17.11	+.04
PeopIn t	14.65	+.06
PeoMid r	15.63	+.06
S&P500R	10.29	+.05
ShIGv	10.61	...
ST Inc p	11.59	...
ShInT p	12.74	+.01
SpGr p	14.51	+.01

Fidelity Advisor:		
EMktA p	8.37	+.64
EqPGr p	28.11	+.19
EqPIA p	15.89	+.04
EqPIB p	15.86	+.04
GblRsc p	15.97	+.04
GovIA p	9.01	+.01
GrOpp p	24.59	+.05
HIMuA p	11.31	+.04
HiYldA p	10.87	...
HiYldB	10.86	...
IncGt p	14.32	+.03
LtTEA p	9.73	+.03
LtTBA p	10.31	...
Ovsea p	12.78	–.10
ST Fi p	9.22	...
StrOpA p	19.53	+.16
Fidelity Invest:		
AgTF r	11.06	+.04
A Mgr	13.72	+.05
AMgrGr	12.52	+.07
AMgrIn	10.48	+.01
Balanc	12.29	+.01
BluCh	25.30	+.07
CA In	9.55	+.06
Canad	14.88	+.09
CapAp	15.77	–.01
CpInc r	8.71	...
CngS	159.51	+
Contra	29.79	+
CnvSc	15.36	+
DestI	14.75	+
DestII	25.08	+
DisEq	17.66	+
DivIntl	10.78	–

QuIG p	11.89	+.03
TelIn p	12.66	+.09
TRTs p	9.31	+.03
Value p	11.40	+.04
Flagship Group:		
AATEa p	10.28	+.04
AATEC p	10.28	+.05
GldRb p	16.56	+.08
IntTE p	9.85	+.03
LtTE p	10.33	+.02
UtilA p	9.77	+.05
Flex Funds:		
Bond p	19.33	+.05
Grth p	13.24	+.05
Muir pf	5.35	–.02
Fortis Funds:		
AstAlA p	14.20	+.04
CapitlA p	17.07	+.10
CaApA p	22.69	+.09
FidcrA p	28.45	+.19
GlbGrA p	13.65	–.01
GvTRA p	7.75	+.02
GrwthA p	25.19	+.21
HiYldA p	7.64	–.01
TFNatE	10.33	+.04
USGvtE	8.72	...
44 WlEq	5.76	+.04
Forum Funds:		

FUNDS FOOTNOTES

e-ex-capital gains distribution.
f-previous day's quotation.
p-fund assets are used to pay distriubtion costs.
r-redemption charge or contingent sales fee may apply.
s-stock dividend or split.
t-both p and r apply.
x-ex-dividend.

Interpreting the Fund Tables

Many newspapers still use the type of presentation shown on page 90. The first column is the NAV, and the second column is the price for investors who bought the fund that day, which means they put in a buy order for the fund before the market closed the day before. If there's an "NL" in the column, the fund is no-load, or at least has no front-end charges. When the number in the buy column is different—it's always greater—than the NAV column, the investor is paying a front-end load.

Figuring out the front-end load is a simple task. It's the difference between the NAV and the price in the buy column. (Sunday papers don't display the buy column.)

Move one column to the right, to the IAI Funds. There's a lowercase "p" next to each fund in that family. In the footnotes, "p" indicates that "fund assets are used to pay distribution costs." This is a 12(b)-1 fund. (For a more complete explanation, see chapter 6.) An "r" indicates a redemption fee. The table doesn't show how much, but if you sell your fund for the NAV listed in the table, you won't collect the full amount. Some no-load funds are listed with an "r," indicating that they charge an exit fee. A "t" in the table tells you that both "p" and "r" apply to this fund.

On occasion, you may see an "x," "e," or "s" listed in the table next to a particular fund. The "x" means the fund just paid a dividend, and investors buying after a certain date won't receive a dividend until the next one. Often such funds decline in NVA, but this is only temporary, reflecting the dividend just paid out of the fund. If a fund pays 10 cents per share, and the price falls 5 cents per share on the ex-dividend date, you can assume the fund would have risen a nickel a share had the dividend not been paid. The "s" works the same as an "x," except it means the dividend is paid in stock instead of cash.

When a fund pays a capital gains distribution, it's listed with the symbol "e" instead of "x." The effect on the fund's share price is the same.

There may be some funds listed with blanks after their names. This usually indicates that the fund company didn't have the price information available when the National Association of Securities Dealers came to collect it. The day after the October 1987 stock market crash, the fund table was strewn with blanks, frightening many investors who thought it showed their funds had been entirely wiped out.

Money-market fund quotes are not usually listed every day. Instead, you can find them on Thursdays (they're released on Wednesdays) and sometimes in Sunday newspapers. Net asset value for money funds is assumed to be held constant at $1 a share—thus, there's no point in reporting it. What is important, however, is the annualized yield for the last 7- and 30-day periods. If it's 2.72 percent—and that's all it was during a recent period—don't assume the fund paid 2.72 percent over the last 7 or 30 days. Instead, it shows that the rate paid during the last 7 or 30 days would amount to 2.72 percent if held constant for a full year. If the 7-day yield is higher than the 30-day yield, interest rates have moved up. If the 7-day yield is less than the 30-day yield, rates have come down.

Average Maturity

Another useful figure in the money-market fund table is average maturity, quoted in days. Consider the $25.9 billion Merrill Lynch CMA Money Fund, the largest fund of its type. At the end of 1993, the fund had a 78-day average maturity, while the Kemper Money Market Portfolio had an average maturity of 44 days. That's a significant difference between the two, particularly if you think short-term interest rates will rise or fall dramatically.

The average maturities of money-market funds are not static. Portfolio managers constantly adjust their average maturities to take advantage of anticipated changes in interest rates, lengthening when rates might fall and shortening when rates might rise.

Keeping track of closed-end funds is a little trickier. You can find the share prices daily under the appropriate stock market listing—New York Stock Exchange, American Stock Exchange, or the NASDAQ National Market System (over-the-counter market). But what you see is the per-share price, which, as you know, is not the same as the net asset value. The NAVs of closed-end funds are usually reported in the financial pages once a week. Closed-end funds usually report NAVs on Fridays, and you can find them in the newspapers over the weekend (Mondays in *The Wall Street Journal* and *Investors Business Daily*).

Keeping Score

It is crucial to remember that the sole purpose of watching your funds' performance is to make sure that they are doing what you *expect* and *want*.

The first thing you probably want to know about a fund is the total return—for the quarter, the year, or some other period. The total return—appreciation plus reinvestment of dividends and capital gains—is one basis on which you can compare a fund's performance to that of a benchmark index like the S&P 500, and also to other funds.

Let's look at Twentieth Century Ultra Investors, a small company fund, as shown in table 8.1. On the first business day of 1989, Ultra had a net asset value of $7 per share. On the last day of the year, the NAV was $8.53. During the year, the fund paid dividends and capital gains distributions amounting to $1.14 per share.

Here's how to figure the fund's return: Start with the final NAV, $8.53. Add in the distributions of $1.14. That brings the total to $9.67. Next, subtract the initial NAV, or $7. That amounts to $2.67, the fund's "profit" for the year. Now divide the $2.67 profit by the starting NAV, $7, which comes to 0.381, or a total return of 38.1 percent.

Table 8.1

How To Compute a Mutual Fund's Return

Twentieth Century Ultra Fund started in 1989 with a net asset value of $7. During the year the fund distributed $1.14 per share to investors. At the end of the year, the NAV was $8.53. What's the fund's total return?

$$\frac{\text{Final NAV} + \text{Distributions} - \text{Starting NAV}}{\text{Starting NAV}} \times 100$$

$$\frac{\$8.53 + \$1.14 - \$7.00}{\$7.00} \times 100$$

$$= \$2.67\ (100) = 0.381 \text{ or } 38.1\%$$

How to Compute Your Return

Suppose you invest $2,000 in a mutual fund and you reinvest the dividends and capital gains distributions of $325. At the end of the year, your account is worth $2,415. In this example you don't need to add in the distributions, they're already included in the current value of your account. If you take the distributions in cash, however, you must add them again, as in the first example.

$$\frac{\text{Current value of shares} - \text{Initial investment}}{\text{Initial investment}} \times 100$$

$$\frac{\$2{,}415 - \$2{,}000}{\$2{,}000} \times 100 = \frac{415\ (100)}{2{,}000}$$

$$=0.208 \text{ or } 20.8\%$$

The method works for any time period, but the key to accurate measurement is to include all distributions.

However, the total return measures how well the portfolio managers performed, not necessarily how well your own investment is doing. For instance, if you paid a load or other charge, that won't be reflected in our total return calculation. So here's a way to calculate your own investment's performance (also shown in table 8.1):

Start with the value of your shares at the end of the period, let's say $2,415 (if the fund has a back-end load or redemption fee that applies to you and you're considering selling the account, you should subtract that from the current value of the shares). If you don't reinvest and you take distributions in cash, add these amounts to your current value figure. Next, subtract your initial investment (any load you paid is already figured in), let's say an even $2,000. Figure the difference, in this case $415, and divide that by the initial investment of $2,000. That yields 0.208, or 20.8 percent.

If you're investing in a mutual fund on a monthly schedule, the calculation becomes a bit more complex. To get an exact return, you need to use a method called the internal rate of return, which accounts for the timing of the investments into the fund. Leave this more detailed calculating to the professionals, or to a computer program that can provide it. You can get a rough approximation of your return by calculating your average cost per share (see "Dollar-Cost Averaging" in chapter 7).

Let's go back to the Twentieth Century Ultra Fund example we used before in table 8.2. Suppose you had invested $200 a month during 1989, for a total of $2,400, and reinvested distributions of $306.23. So you have $2,706.23 in the investment, and you own 303.654 shares. Dividing the number of dollars by the number of shares yields an average cost per share of $8.91. At mid-year, 1990, the NAV was $9.48, so you could say your investment gained 57 cents a share in the first six months of 1990, or 6.4 percent. However, by the beginning of December 1990, the NAV was down to $8.85, so your 1989 investment was showing a loss of six cents a share.

Do all these numbers have you breaking out in a cold sweat? Calm yourself! With a little patience, plus a pocket calculator, a pencil, and paper, you can sort it all out quite easily.

Let the Computer Do It

While a computer is not absolutely essential to keep track of your mutual funds, if you do have a personal computer and are willing to take the time to master new software, there are a number of money and investment management programs that simplify the "keeping-up" process. The programs allow an investor to set up multiple portfolios: yours, your spouse's, the IRAs, and the kids', for example, each with an unlimited number of investments. You can also treat each mutual fund as a portfolio.

Fund investors might find it convenient to organize portfolios by the fund family—like Fidelity or Franklin—or by the broker who handles the account—like Dean Witter or PaineWebber. Computer power is particularly handy for investors who make frequent purchases and regular reinvestments of dividends and capital gains. If you invest monthly and reinvest the income and distributions, you will be making 12 to 16 transactions a year. By entering each one into the computer program, you'll easily be able to determine how many shares of each investment you have, what they're worth, and your average cost per share. More important, the programs show each transaction individually as well as the profit or loss on particular investments.

Suppose an overall investment is in the black, but several purchases of funds were made at higher prices and are now in the red. The right program will flag those transactions, which is particularly helpful for tax planning purposes (more on this in chapter 9).

A listing of the many financial software packages available is shown in table 8.2. The two best known—Andrew Tobias's Managing Your Money and Quicken—are appreciated primarily for their check writing, bill paying, and household-budgeting features. Both packages also have portfolio functions and are better with each successive version manufactured. (Prices of these packages have been coming down because of heavy discounting.)

Managing Your Money goes well beyond record keeping, offering fairly sophisticated investment analysis and asset allocation features. Quicken is not as sophisticated with financial planning, but it's generally considered easier to use—or at least to learn. Either personal financial software package will do a fine job with portfolio management.

If you use one of these programs only to manage your portfolio, you're paying for many features you don't use, so you may prefer WealthBuilder by *Money Magazine*. This is strictly a personal financial planning and investment management program and therefore may be the easiest of the three to use for personal portfolio management.

The "Mercedes" of personal finance programs for the individual investor is Smart Investor by *Money Magazine*. It not only provides personal investment software but also interacts with scads of data and investment research reports accessed through an on-line service. You'll need a modem to take advantage of all its features, including entering orders through discount brokers.

Many people don't want or need the bells and whistles of a program like Smart Investor. If you need a system for record keeping only, CompuVest is an excellent choice. Developed by Jones & Babson, a mutual fund management company, CompuVest has a nifty feature that will be invaluable at tax time: It can calculate your "cost basis" the three different ways that are accepted by the IRS (more on this in chapter 9), allowing you to select the one that's most advantageous.

In contrast, Kiplinger's CA-Simply Money, a new entry in personal finance software, uses only one method.

If you are already familiar with spreadsheet programs such as Lotus 1-2-3, Microsoft Excel, or Quattro Pro, you can use them to design your own record-keeping system.

If you are a charting aficionado, Mutual Fund Investor, a program from American River Software, has some snazzy features, such as one that zooms in on a fund's performance in select periods of time. (Is a particular 17-day trading period of interest to you?) Fundmaster TC, a program from Time Trend Software, also combines portfolio management and technical charting tools you can customize.

If you want to know the performance of thousands of mutual funds, there's the *Business Week* Mutual Fund Scoreboard on diskettes. Scoreboard diskettes, updated monthly, allow users to screen the data for funds with particular characteristics such as a minimum total return, a maximum sales charge, or a low expense ratio. The diskette scoreboard has more than 1,700 equity funds and another 1,700 fixed-income funds. New funds are added each month.

Table 8.2

Keeping Track the Computerized Way

Available Through Retailers and Mail Order

Lotus 1-2-3 Home, $69.95
Lotus Development Corporation
55 Cambridge Parkway, Cambridge, MA 02142
Phone: 800-343-5414

Andrew Tobias's Managing Your Money, $39.95
MECA Software
Box 907, Westport, CT 06430
Phone: 203-256-5000

Quattro Pro, $49.95
Borland International
Box 660001, Scotts Valley, CA 95067
Phone 800-331-0877

Quicken, $69.95
Intuit Software
Box 3014, Menlo Park, CA 94026
Phone: 800-624-8742

Wealthbuilder by *Money Magazine*, $69.95
Reality's Smart Investor by *Money Magazine*, $49.95
Reality Technologies
3624 Market Street, Philadelphia, PA 19104
Phone: 800-346-2024

Mail Order Only

Business Week Mutual Fund Scoreboard
Box 1597, 185 Bridge Plaza North, Suite 302
Fort Lee, NJ 07024
Phone: 800-553-3575

CompuVest, $29.95
Jones & Babson
Three Crown Center
2440 Pershing Road, Kansas City, MO 64108
Phone: 800-422-2766

Fund Master TC, $289
Time Trend Software
337 Boston Road, Billerica, MA 08121
Phone: 508-663-3330

Mutual Fund Decision Aide, $49
V. A. Denslow & Associates
4151 Woodland Avenue, Western Spring, IL 60558
Phone: 312-246-3365

Mutual Fund Investor, $295.95
American River Software
1523 Kingsford Drive, Carmichael, CA 95608
Phone: 916-483-1600

For the Most Complete Catalog of Investment Software

The Individual Investor's Guide to Computerized Investing, $24.95

American Assocation of Individual Investors
625 N. Michigan Avenue, Chicago, IL 60611
Phone: 312-280-0170

When Your Fund Is Ailing

Suppose you notice that one of your fund's performance is slipping. The long-term record is still exceptional, and you're a long-term investor, so you stick with the fund—and watch it slip away. Now you're losing real money. What do you do?

This is the most difficult question in all of investing: When do you jettison a fund that's in a funk? You could sell at the very bottom of the decline.

Maybe you paid a load to get into the fund and are reluctant to leave right now. Sometimes people just refuse to admit they made a bad investment—there's too much ego involved—so they're often slow to sell when they should.

Before pushing the "sell" button on a poorly performing fund, it's a good idea to ask some pertinent questions about it. The most important is: How is the fund doing relative to its market sector and peer group? Suppose the S&P 500 delivered a total return of 10 percent over the previous period, and your growth-and-income fund gained only half that much. See how much better the other growth-and-income funds performed. If your fund did well among its peer group, you know the problem is strategic—with the *group*—rather than solely with your particular fund.

If you had owned a junk bond fund in the latter half of 1989 and into 1990, you may have been dismayed by plunging net asset values. At that time, no junk fund was looking good. You may have owned one of the better junk bond funds, but you couldn't know that until you compared performance within the entire group.

Knowing the entire group is in trouble, you may choose to sell out, but you'll be too savvy to replace your fund with another of the same kind. However, if you're attracted by the long-term results of these types of funds, you might stick with them through good times and bad.

It's also useful to assess your motivation in choosing this investment. If you were trying to seize upon a trading opportunity—whether rising interest rates, a declining dollar, or something else—you can re-evaluate to see if the opportunity still exists. But if you bought to diversify your portfolio, chances are some of your other diversified investments are doing better, so you might be inclined to hold on a while longer.

In evaluating a mutual fund, remember that few funds do well under all market conditions. Instead of steady gains in all economic conditions, look for bigger gains in the up periods than losses in the down periods.

Another reason to dump a fund is that it's no longer doing the job you expected it to do. Ask the professionals who advise pension funds on selection of investment managers: The only sin worse than underperforming the market is not following your stated investment program.

In short, don't dump a fund on performance alone. Compare your fund to an appropriate market index, like the S&P 500, the S&P MidCap 400, or, for small-cap stocks, the Russell 2000. Compare the fund to its peer group as well.

Keeping in Touch with Your Fund

When you buy a mutual fund you are, in effect, "hiring" an investment manager. So one aspect of overseeing your fund portfolio is making sure your fund managers are doing what they told you they would do. If, for example, you invest in a small-company fund, you don't want the manager buying stocks in IBM, AT&T, and GE.

Funds do change gears, of course, but they're supposed to notify you. As a shareholder, you're entitled to get regular reports—at least semiannually, although many report quarterly as well. Funds have 90 days after the close of their fiscal accounting periods (6 months and 12 months) to deliver shareholder reports. These reports can be very educational, even though the information may be quite dated by the time you see it.

Shareholder reports vary in their content and presentation. The Gintel Fund, for instance, has a very simple

Table 8.3

GINTEL FUND

Status of Investments

September 30, 1993
(Unaudited)

COMMON STOCKS		PURCHASE COST	MARKET VALUE	PER SHARE COST	PER SHARE MARKET	% OF NET ASSETS
952,500	Amtech*	15,370,365	26,789,063	16.76	28.13	18.6
200,000	Federal National Mortgage	11,310,601	15,750,000	56.55	78.75	10.9
150,000	American President Co.	6,466,626	7,200,000	43.11	48.00	5.0
100,000	Schering-Plough Corp.	5,171,340	6,587,500	51.71	65.88	4.6
150,000	Union Camp	6,726,440	6,356,250	44.84	42.38	4.4
600,000	MTC Electronics	5,850,000	6,150,000	9.75	10.25	4.3
150,000	Capstead Mortgage	2,932,500	5,850,000	19.55	39.00	4.1
600,000	Checkpoint Systems	5,283,046	5,775,000	8.81	9.63	4.0
665,000	Oneita Industries	8,414,133	4,322,500	12.65	6.50	3.0
100,000	Phelps Dodge*	(4,065,422)	3,975,000	19.25	39.75	2.8
127,500	FirstFed Michigan Corp.	1,147,750	3,267,188	9.00	25.63	2.3
150,000	Santa Fe Pacific	2,108,125	2,737,500	14.05	18.25	1.9
200,000	Vertex, Inc.	3,100,800	2,650,000	15.50	13.25	1.8
273,300	Magma Copper	1,565,870	2,459,700	5.73	9.00	1.7
285,000	Genesco	1,147,825	2,280,000	4.03	8.00	1.6
350,000	Chart Industries	3,555,926	2,143,750	10.16	6.13	1.5
352,000	Hexcel Corp.	3,604,772	2,112,000	10.24	6.00	1.5
350,000	Terra Industries Inc.	1,703,248	1,662,500	4.87	4.75	1.1
	Miscellaneous Securities	6,902,891	7,377,165			5.1
	Total Investments	$88,296,836	115,445,115			80.2
	Cash and Short-Term Investments		28,555,150			19.8
	NET ASSETS		**$144,000,265**			100.0
	NET ASSET VALUE PER SHARE		**$16.60**			
	INCREASE IN NET ASSET VALUE PER SHARE YEAR-TO-DATE		**0.9%**			

*Net of Short Sales

but informative report as shown in table 8.3. All fund reports will show the market value of a security on the day of the report, but Gintel's also discloses the purchase price of the investment, essentially a line-by-line report card on how the fund manager is doing.

The Gintel Fund lists its stocks in the order of their total value within the portfolio. Amtech, a manufacturer of electronic identification products, is by far the largest holding, with 952,000 shares worth $26,789,063. Compared with the purchase cost of these shares, $15,370,365, you can see that the fund has a tidy profit in this stock. If you find thinking in millions is a little unwieldy, use the per-share cost and market value that Gintel also reports.

By disclosing its costs, this fund also reveals its losing positions—stocks whose market value is now below what the fund paid. By looking for cost higher than present market value, you find 6 of the fund's 18 holdings are in the red.

This cost information isn't in every fund's reports. Typically, funds report only the name of the security and its market value on the date of the report. The American Funds group, for instance, doesn't provide the shareholder's costs but otherwise does a good job in portfolio reporting. Look at table 8.4, from the 1993 Annual Report of the SMALLCAP World Fund. At the top, there's summary information on major investment categories, industries, and the

Table 8.4

SMALLCAP World Fund

INVESTMENT PORTFOLIO September 30, 1993

Largest Investment Categories	Percent of Net Assets
Services	35.83%
Capital Equipment	18.41
Finance	10.15

Largest Industry Holdings	Percent of Net Assets
Broadcasting & Publishing	9.99
Merchandising	8.45
Telecommunications	6.70
Banking	5.93
Data Processing & Reproduction	5.56

Largest Individual Holdings	Percent of Net Assets
Liberty Media	3.06%
Lands' End	1.29
Tolmex	1.28
BayBanks	1.14
Consolidated Stores	1.14
Associated Communications	1.13
Washington Mutual Savings Bank	1.10
Gaylord Entertainment	1.01
Cablevision Systems	1.00
Corel	.92

Equity-Type Securities *(common and preferred stocks and convertible debentures)*		*Shares or Principal Amount*	*Market Value (000)*	*Percent of Net Assets*
ENERGY				
Energy Sources — 2.44%	*Ampolex Ltd., 8.00% convertible preferred (Australia)* Explores for and develops oil and natural gas fields primarily in Australia and other Pacific Basin nations as well as in Latin America.	908,000	$ 3,512	.16%
	Ashland Coal, Inc. (USA)[1] Mines low-sulphur coal, sold primarily to utilities in the eastern U.S. and Europe.	330,000	9,817	.44
	Cabre Exploration Ltd. (Canada)[2] Rapidly growing Canadian oil company with substantial oil and gas reserves, an excellent exploration record and minimal debt.	407,000	4,570	.20
	California Energy Co., Inc. (USA)[2] Converts geothermal resources into electrical power for sale to public utilities. Well positioned to benefit from government environmental regulations and incentives.	350,000	6,431	.29
	Chieftain International, Inc. (Canada)[2] Primarily involved in natural gas exploration and development in the United States, with additional oil and gas activities in the North Sea.	50,000	925	.04
	ELAN Energy Inc. (Canada)[2]	1,235,000	12,710	.64
	ELAN Energy Inc., warrants, expire 1993[2] Formerly LASMO Canada Inc., ELAN participates in oil and natural gas exploration and production and seeks acquisitions to expand its reserves.	400,000	1,534	
	Elf Gabon SA (Gabon) The leading oil company in Gabon, West Africa, the smallest member of OPEC.	6,700	1,210	.05
	Flextech PLC (United Kingdom) Holding company for subsidiaries providing television programs and cable TV services.	1,700,000	3,711	.16
	Jordan Petroleum Ltd., Class A (Canada) Engaged in exploration and development of oil and natural gas reserves throughout Canada.	450,000	3,284	.15
	Northstar Energy Corp. (Canada)[2] Oil and gas company with reserves concentrated in western Canada.	78,000	1,650	.07
	OESI Power Corp. (USA)[2] Develops and operates geothermal power projects in the western U.S. using exclusive licensed technology that generates electricity efficiently and prolongs the life of the geothermal source.	170,000	297	.01
	Paramount Resources Ltd. (Canada) A specialized natural gas producer that develops shallow, low-pressure reservoirs in northeastern Alberta. Has significant reserves and is noted for proven management and low development costs.	300,000	5,165	.23

fund's ten largest holdings. Without reading any further, the shareholder can see how his or her money is invested. More than one-third (35.83 percent) is invested in service companies, while broadcasting and publishing represents nearly 10 percent of the portfolio. Liberty Media is the largest single holding.

If you want more information, there's plenty to follow. Look down the page. The first broad category is "Energy," and under that is listed "Energy Sources." Here you'll find the fund's individual holdings, including number of shares and market value, translated into dollars. Since SMALLCAP World is a global fund, the report identifies the home base of each company. There's also a brief description of each company's business.

Most reports include a letter to shareholders from the president of the fund management company or from the portfolio manager. This letter typically discusses market conditions, although by the time you get the report things may have changed dramatically.

Twice a year, the fund is supposed to provide you with a complete list of its holdings. You shouldn't try to second-guess the portfolio manager, but a quick scan might be quite revealing. If the fund is supposed to invest in small, fast-growing companies and you don't recognize many of the companies' names, then the fund manager is probably pursuing what he or she promised. If, however, you have a high-quality bond fund and you find it's peppered with junk bonds, you ought to ask a few questions. Don't be bashful. Call the fund management company and ask for explanation of anything you find amiss or don't understand.

Overall, the quality of shareholder reports varies widely. Some fund managers are brutally frank when they have had a period of bad performance; others are elliptical or evasive, and never admit poor results head-on. Others, still, are more open in their disclosure of performance.

John B. Neff, who runs the Vanguard/Windsor Fund, includes a report card on his performance by comparing it to that of his fund's major holdings against their industry groups. For instance, in a recent annual report, Neff gave himself *A*'s for investments in banks, building and construction, conglomerates, data processing, and telephone companies. Neff's Citicorp investment, for example, was up 118 percent versus 17.7 percent for the industry group. But he gave himself a C for his chemical investments, most of which trailed the industry index, and a D for investments in nonferrous metals.

Morningstar, Inc., the mutual fund information company, also studies shareholder reports. Morningstar's analysts look at the amount of financial information—above and beyond what's required by law—and the presentation. Is it organized in a reader-friendly manner? Can the shareholder learn something about the investment from the reports? Morningstar discovered that good funds don't necessarily earn *A*'s and *B*'s on their reports, but poor performers rarely have great reports. In general, Morningstar discovered a positive correlation between superior equity-fund shareholder reports and the returns these funds achieve.

In a recent study, for instance, Morningstar rated the shareholder reports of 45 funds an *A*, and found these funds had five-year average annual returns of 20.8 percent. Funds with reports they rated *B* had an 18.1 percent average annual return for the same five-year period. Funds with reports rated *B*– through *D* all produced returns of about 15.5 percent. Only six fund reports flunked, and these funds returned only 4.7 percent to their investors.

The periodic reports should not be your only communication from a fund. Every time the prospectus is updated, you should get a new copy for your files. When a major policy change occurs, such as imposition of a load or a 12(b)-1 fee, or a change in redemption procedures, you should receive notification by letter. You may also receive invitations to the fund's annual corporate meetings, proxy statements, and ballots allowing you to vote on matters such as elections of fund directors, hiring of auditors, changes in fees or sales charges, and other fund business.

Don't toss out these proxies or ballots—not even seemingly innocuous ones. You don't have to vote yes, and you can indicate that you want to abstain from voting. But sign and return the proxy statement in the postage-paid envelope because your funds need a quorum to hold their meetings. If a fund fails to obtain enough proxies for a quorum, it will have to conduct another mailing, at extra cost to you and other shareholders.

By signing the proxy, you give persons named on the statement the

T.RowePrice

U.S. Treasury Money Fund

We Need Your Proxy Vote Before June 13, 1991.

Detach card at perforation and mail in postage paid envelope provided.

PROXY — T. ROWE PRICE U.S. TREASURY FUNDS, INC. — PROXY

U.S. TREASURY MONEY FUND
ANNUAL MEETING OF SHAREHOLDERS — JUNE 13, 1991
THIS PROXY IS SOLICITED ON BEHALF OF THE BOARD OF DIRECTORS

The undersigned hereby appoints George J. Collins and Edward A. Taber, III, as proxies, each with the power to appoint his substitute, and hereby authorizes them to represent and to vote, as designated below, all shares of stock of U.S. TREASURY MONEY FUND, which the undersigned is entitled to vote at the Annual Meeting of Shareholders to be held on Thursday, June 13, 1991, at 11:00 o'clock a.m., Eastern time, at the offices of the Corporation, 100 East Pratt Street, Baltimore, Maryland 21202, and at any and all adjournments thereof, with respect to the matters set forth below and described in the Notice of Annual Meeting and Proxy Statement dated April 25, 1991, receipt of which is hereby acknowledged.

1. Ratify the selection of the firm of Price Waterhouse as independent accountants. ☐ For ☐ Against ☐ Abstain 1.
2. Approve a new Investment Management Agreement between the Fund and T. Rowe Price Associates, Inc. ☐ For ☐ Against ☐ Abstain 2.
3. Amend the Fund's Articles of Incorporation to remove the requirement that stock certificates of the Fund be issued to Fund shareholders requesting them. ☐ For ☐ Against ☐ Abstain 3.
4. In their discretion, the Proxies are authorized to vote upon such other business as may properly come before the meeting.

legal right to vote your shares as you direct. You get one vote for each share, but a single signature authorizes the voting of all your shares.

When the Fund Manager Changes

One of the toughest questions in mutual fund investing is what to do when the portfolio manager changes, especially "star" managers like Peter Lynch, who piloted the Fidelity Magellan Fund to tremendous successes and took an early retirement from fund management in 1990. Of course, Lynch's departure was big news. It's often more difficult to determine if your fund's manager has left.

One way is to pay close attention. The management company now must disclose the change of managers somewhere in the fund's documents. Another way is to ask at regular intervals.

How much a change of leadership actually matters depends on the type and structure of the fund. With money-market and even many bond funds, one manager is unlikely to do much better than another. Some fund management companies, such as the American Funds and Twentieth Century Investors, use a team approach to investment management, so any one portfolio manager may hardly be missed.

In equity funds, however, the manager has much greater latitude. When Peter Lynch retired from the Fidelity Magellan Fund, mutual fund analysts were split over whether to sell. Six months after Lynch's departure, those who sold looked smart. Just weeks after Morris Smith took over the reins, the stock market headed down. Magellan underperformed the falling market, but the fund is so large and owns so many stocks that its performance in the second half of 1990 may have been inevitable, regardless of who was at the helm. In 1991 the stock market rallied, and so did Magellan, rising 41 percent for the year.

When Smith left the fund early in 1992, his successor, Jeff Vinik, came in with an excellent track record (he formerly ran Fidelity Contrafund and Fidelity Growth & Income Fund) and helped Magellan post a 24.7 percent total annual return, more than doubling the return of the S&P 500 during the same period.

Neither Lynch's nor Smith's departure was fatal for Magellan because Fidelity has an exceptional pool of managerial talent and an army of equally talented research analysts. In fact, the company changes fund managers fairly frequently—and with few problems.

Still, many investment managers and financial planners switch funds when a well-regarded fund manager leaves. There have been no definitive studies yet, but Morningstar uncovered some interesting anecdotal evidence in late 1990. It looked at five "star" managers who switched funds and measured how their old funds had done versus their new funds since the switch. In all five cases, investors following the manager to the new fund would have done better.

But there's anecdotal evidence to the contrary as well. Donald Yacktman built an enviable record with Selected American Fund but left in early 1992 to set up the Yacktman Fund. His reputation was enough to draw in $70 million or so in the first six months, a decent start considering Yacktman did not have a large fund company behind him. But in his first full year of operation, the new fund lost 6.6 percent.

In late 1993, Pioneering Management, the company which manages the Pioneer family of funds, took over five Mutual of Omaha funds and, in all but one muni bond fund, installed its own portfolio managers. In such a case, it's advisable to inquire as to what other funds your new manager has run and to check out his performance history.

Mutual Fund Mergers

For the most part, when a fund does a reasonable job of meeting its investment objectives, the management company doesn't tinker with success. Poorly performing funds or funds in poorly performing sectors of the stock market, however, are far more likely to get a makeover, including merging the weaker fund with a stronger one. Generally, in mergers, the track records of the losers vanish and are replaced with the track record of the fund surviving the merger.

It's common to merge several funds within the same fund family into one new fund, or to add a smaller, less successful fund to a larger, more successful one. Small, poorly performing funds are merger candidates because they are in a catch-22 situation. Being small, they tend to have higher overhead and expense ratios, which cut into their total returns. Without strong returns, they are not able to attract

Portfolio management is often done in teams, allowing for less confusion if a manager leaves the firm or takes on additional clients.

enough new investments to overcome their size disadvantage.

During 1991, Oppenheimer Management Corporation was a hotbed of mutual fund mergers. The company merged its Ninety-Ten and Premium Income funds—both of which used options to generate income, albeit not too successfully—into its Oppenheimer Asset Allocation Fund, which attempts to maintain steady growth and a regular dividend stream. In this case, the investment objectives of the surviving fund were not significantly different from those of the merged funds. In a like manner, Oppenheimer merged two laggard growth stock funds, Directors and Regency, into the better-performing Oppenheimer Target Fund.

Transamerica Funds went this route, too, adding the Lowry Market Timing, Special Global Growth, and Sunbelt Growth funds to the more successful Transamerica Special Emerging Growth Fund.

In early 1990, the Vanguard Group merged its Explorer and Explorer II funds (technology funds), and with the approval of shareholders changed the investment objective of the new, combined fund to invest in emerging growth companies. This dismayed some shareholders who invested in Explorer because of its technological bent, but if Explorer had been successful as originally established, Vanguard wouldn't have changed it. Vanguard also merged the poorly performing Vanguard High-Yield Stock Fund into its Vanguard/Windsor Fund. In this case, merged shareholders found themselves in a fund with a slightly more aggressive investment posture, a somewhat better track record, and a portfolio 100 times as large. One commonality was apparent, though: John Neff ran both funds.

Whenever there is a fund merger, shareholders get new fund shares to replace the old one in a tax-free exchange. If you don't want to go along with the shift, you should vote against it; if it passes anyway, start looking for another fund with objectives and a track record closer to what you want.

Change Objectives, Change Funds

Every investor's objectives, ability to assume risks, and income needs change over time—usually in a gradual and predictable way. Sometimes, however, the changes are abrupt, as when you unexpectedly lose your job or suffer health problems. When your investment objectives change, you might find that your maximum-growth fund, while profitable, is no longer an appropriate investment.

Changes in tax status may also dictate a shift in funds. As your income increases, so does the relative attractiveness of tax-exempt bond and money-market funds. Once in retirement, when tax rates are usually lower, you might once again find taxable bond funds more attractive.

You needn't accommodate these shifts all at once, and in fact you might best accomplish them in stages. If moving funds results in a capital gains tax liability, for example, you might want to spread the move out over several tax years.

Chapter 9

Taxes and Record Keeping

Tempted as you may be to ignore or throw away the confirmation notices and other financial statements you get from your mutual funds, *don't!* When you sell later on, these records will be essential for tax purposes.

Each time you make an investment in a fund, you'll receive a statement from the fund management company (see table 9.1). It will show the date and amount of the investment, the dollar price per share, the number of shares purchased, and the total number of shares in the fund. Redemptions trigger more paper. Switch $1,000 dollars from, say, a long-term bond fund to a money-market fund, and you may get three statements: one from the bond fund showing the redemption of shares, one from the money-market fund showing a new investment, and another from the fund management company indicating that an exchange has taken place.

If you're making monthly investments as part of your dollar-cost averaging program, you'll receive 12 statements a year. But if your fund issues "cumulative" statements, by

Table 9.1

Investment Account Statement / 1989 CALENDAR YEAR

THE Vanguard GROUP OF INVESTMENT COMPANIES

EUGENE H SCHILLINGER
8125 OAK LANE
NORRISTOWN PA 19403

CURRENT ACCOUNT SUMMARY
AUGUST 14, 1989
SHARES OWNED 1,655.984
SHARE PRICE $ 12.16
ACCOUNT VALUE $20,136.76

Vanguard
MUNICIPAL BOND FUND
Intermediate-Term Portfolio

Tele-Account No. 42
For Account Service
Call Toll-Free 1-800-662-2003

Account No. 456789012-3
Social Security or
Tax ID No. 123-45-6789

When writing to Vanguard, please include your fund name and account number and mail to:
THE VANGUARD GROUP
P.O. BOX 1103 * VALLEY FORGE, PA 19482-1103

Trade Date	Transaction Description	Dollar Amount	Share Price	Share Amount	Shares Owned
	BEGINNING BALANCE				1,433.565
1/13	SHARES PURCHASED	325.00	11.94	27.219	1,460.784
1/26	SHARES PURCHASED	152.50	12.01	12.698	1,473.482
2/01	INCOME REINVEST	101.06	12.02	8.408	1,481.890
2/08	SHARES PURCHASED	375.00	12.00	31.250	1,513.140
3/01	INCOME REINVEST	104.47	11.85	8.816	1,521.956
4/03	INCOME REINVEST	106.92	11.76	9.092	1,531.048
4/11	SHARES PURCHASED	175.00	11.81	14.818	1,545.866
5/01	INCOME REINVEST	107.27	11.95	8.977	1,554.843
6/01	INCOME REINVEST	109.23	12.09	9.035	1,563.878
6/02	SHARES PURCHASED	350.00	12.12	28.878	1,592.756
7/03	INCOME REINVEST	113.64	12.15	9.353	1,602.109
8/01	INCOME REINVEST	115.79	12.24	9.460	1,611.569
8/14	SHARES PURCHASED	540.09	12.16	44.415	1,655.984

PAID THIS CALENDAR YEAR	Taxable Income	or	Tax Exempt Income	+	Short-Term Gains	+	Long-Term Gains	=	TOTAL DISTRIBUTIONS
			758.38						758.38

December you should have the entire year's transactions on one piece of paper. Feel free to slim down your files by tossing out the previous 11 months' statements.

Other transactions generate paper, too. Each time the fund pays a dividend or capital gains distribution, it puts another statement in the mail. Many bond and some stock funds, like the fund shown in table 9.1, make distributions monthly. If you are making monthly investments in a fund that makes distributions monthly, you can imagine the paper that's piling up. It's enough to make you want to buy growth-oriented equity funds, since most of them make distributions only once a year.

Now imagine a fund in which you invested on several occasions at various prices, whose shares you sold a few times, also at various prices, and whose distributions you reinvested, again at various prices. You have tons of paper to keep track of. Even a computer won't stop the blizzard. A good software program will help you keep track of the information and make it more manageable. But the postal service is going to continue delivering the statements, so you'll have to enter the information on each of them properly into the program.

But your biggest headache isn't paper—it's taxes.

Mutual Funds' Special Tax Status

A set of rules govern how mutual funds (and also closed-end funds) must behave to keep their special tax status. It's up to you, however, as the shareholder to keep track of everything you send to and receive from the fund. If you miss reporting a dividend or capital gains distribution, you're likely to get a letter from the IRS and a bill for the taxes due—plus interest and a penalty.

Fortunately, the funds send out 1099-DIV forms telling you exactly how much you received during the year, plus 1099-B forms detailing the proceeds from any sales of fund shares.

Sometimes you'll owe taxes, but other times you may have a paper loss you can apply as a deduction against other investment gains. Bottom line: Without good records, you'll never know what to do at tax time.

Here's a brief overview of mutual fund investments and their tax implications: Most mutual funds are also corporations, and shareholders of corporations, in effect, pay tax twice. The corporation pays taxes on its earnings, and, if it pays any of these earnings to its shareholders as dividends, the shareholders pay taxes on them as income. Mutual funds escape this double taxation. The fund is treated as a "conduit," passing all its income and the responsibility for paying taxes on it to its shareholders.

To keep their special tax status, mutual funds must adhere to rigorous rules. For instance, a fund can't hold more than 10 percent of the outstanding voting stock in any one company.

There's also what's known as the "short-short" rule: No more than 30 percent of a fund's gross income can come from securities held for less than 90 days. For example, the Smith Barney Shearson Sector Analysis Fund ran afoul of this a few years ago. The fund had opened for business in 1987 and made a splashy debut. Not only did it sidestep the market crash, but Elaine Garzarelli, the fund's manager and Shearson's top market strategist, had also purchased put options that soared in value as the market tanked. Garzarelli quickly sold the options and reaped significant short-term gains. The gains were so great that the fund ended up violating the short-short rule. So for that fiscal year, the fund ended up having to pay tax that nicked about 15 cents off the fund's NAV.

Mutual funds have been living under yet another set of requirements since the 1986 tax act. Prior to that, funds could take profits in December and make distributions in January. That way, the tax on the distribution would not be due until April 15 of the following year, essentially giving shareholders a 15-month no-interest loan from the government. To stop this tax deferral, funds must now distribute 98 percent of their income and dividends—in the calendar year they are earned. In addition, the funds must distribute 98 percent of their net realized capital gains—both short- and long-term. If the funds fail to meet these distribution tests, they can be hit with a 4 percent tax on the undistributed income.

As with other investment income, not all distributions from a mutual fund are taxed equally. You'll pay your regular rate on mutual fund distributions of dividends, interest income, and short-term capital gains—and that can be as high as 39.6 percent. Long-term capital gains generated by investments held in the mutual fund for more than one year are taxed at a maximum rate of 28 percent.

How much a fund distributes in income and capital gains has a direct bearing on your after-tax return. Suppose two mutual funds generate the same pretax total return. The first fund made no income or capital gains distributions to shareholders, because it didn't own dividend-bearing stocks and tended to hold rather than trade the stocks in the portfolio. All its net gain is therefore long-term capital gains. The second fund produced the same total return, but about half of it was in the form of distributions of dividends and short-term gains to shareholders. Since you'd pay more taxes on the profits made in the second mutual fund, the first fund would give you a higher after-tax return.

Of course, if you hold the fund in an IRA or other tax-deferred plan, the relative tax rates on its distributions and profits aren't as significant, but if you're going to pay current taxes on a fund's profit performance, its history and policy of making distributions *is* a real concern.

Many funds, especially those that practice a buy-and-hold investment strategy, often carry huge unrealized and undistributed capital gains. Morningstar, for example, measures these gains and expresses their magnitude as a percentage of the fund's total holdings. Suppose a fund's portfolio contains 30 percent unrealized capital gains. If the fund were liquidated at $10 a share, $3 of that would be "realized" and taxable to shareholders as capital gain. Some investors are wary of funds with relatively large untaxed gains because they don't want to pay tax on capital gains that were earned before they bought into the fund. However, they're perfectly willing to buy funds in the opposite position.

Sometimes mutual funds have realized net losses rather than gains. Tax rules do not allow mutual funds to distribute their losses to their shareholders, but the funds can carry the losses forward for eight years and deduct them against future taxable gains (many precious metals funds and some junk bond funds are in this position). As these markets recover, existing losses will reduce their shareholders' tax liabilities on future gains. Provided a fund meets all your other criteria, investing in a fund with existing tax losses gives you a chance to shelter any new gains from taxes.

Mutual fund companies usually mail form 1099-DIVs to shareholders by the end of January. This form reports dividend, nontaxable, and capital gains distributions—broken out to show both short-term and long-term—and taxes paid to foreign governments, if any, which are more common with international funds.

The numbers you see on the form are the same numbers that the IRS is going to see, so check the figures against your own records and verify their accuracy.

Distribution Dates

It's a good idea to start checking with funds around Thanksgiving to ask about upcoming distributions. A customer service representative will usually know if a distribution is planned. Some will even give you an estimate of the date and amount, although you may have to call back until you can get the details. The funds themselves often don't know the date and size of the distribution until very late in the year. Sometimes the fund management company will simply announce the exact date and the per-share distribution rate.

You'll want to be cautious about purchasing shares right before distribution dates, since this could dilute your new investment with profits that you earned long before (see chapter 7).

Tax Swaps

Some investors like to do "tax swapping" at the end of a tax year. The term comes from the bond market but can apply to any investment. The idea is to look for a fund in which you may have an unrealized loss and then sell the fund to take the loss and generate a tax deduction. At the same time, you move the money into a mutual fund with characteristics similar to the one just sold (see table 9.2). This way, you get the tax advantages of your loss while keeping your investment program in place.

Swapping within the same fund family is easiest. Load-fund investors who swap within their fund groups may save some money, and large fund families often have several funds with similar objectives, such as the Fidelity Growth Company Fund and the Fidelity Magellan Fund—both growth funds. Fidelity Equity-Income and Equity-Income II, as their names might suggest, are also interchangeable. Twentieth Century Funds' growth funds are good swap candidates.

Table 9.2

Saving on Taxes by Swapping Funds

If you have a loss in a mutual fund, you may want to sell it for a tax loss. If so, you may want to shift the money into a similar fund so as not to change your investment goals. The funds within each grouping below have similar investment policies and risk profiles. They can make suitable swaps.

Funds	Comments
Fidelity Growth Company Fidelity Magellan Janus Janus Growth & Income	Growth Company is probably the most like Magellan for those who want to switch under the Fidelity umbrella. Likewise, the Janus funds are similar enough to do the same.
Fidelity Equity-Income Fidelity Equity-Income II Invesco Industrial Income T. Rowe Price Equity-Income	Clone funds can make good swap candidates. Equity-income funds are fairly uniform compared to growth and maximum-growth funds, which are far more diverse in their investment practices and have a greater variation in returns.
Fidelity Emerging Markets Lexington Worldwide Emerging Markets T. Rowe Price International Scudder International	The two emerging markets funds, though offered by different companies, should be similar enough for tax swapping. The Price and Scudder international funds have similar portfolio characteristics.
Templeton Growth Templeton Value Templeton World	Many Templeton equity funds are interchangeable. The developing markets, foreign, real estate, and small-company funds are unique, however.
Babson Enterprise II Evergreen Nicholas II Royce Value	These small-company funds lean toward "value" investing, with prosaic rather than cutting-edge companies, but they can make money for investors.
AIM Constellation AIM Weingarten Twentieth Century Ultra Investors Berger 100	These funds comb the markets for companies with earnings momentum, then hang on as long as earnings growth continues. The AIM funds are load, Berger and Twentieth Century, no-load.
Babson Bond Fidelity Intermediate Bond Vanguard Bond Market	Swapping bond funds is easier than equity funds, since these funds have easily identifiable characteristics, such as maturity and credit quality.
Invesco High-Yield T. Rowe Price High-Yield Vanguard Fixed-Income High-Yield	All high-yield, or junk, bond funds are not alike. These all invest in better-quality junk bonds.

Some advisers discourage investors from swapping funds purely for tax purposes. If a swap triggers redemption fees or new sales charges, the costs can greatly reduce the anticipated benefit from the trade. On the other hand, if you can justify selling one fund and buying another as a good investment decision, then saving a little extra on taxes is an attractive sweetener to the swap.

What's My "Cost Basis"?

Mention the term "cost basis," and eyes glaze over, but it's really quite a

A broker can assist you in figuring the cost basis of your investments.

simple concept. Your cost basis is just the money you put into an investment. If you buy 100 shares of stock at $40 per share and pay the broker a $50 commission, your cost basis is $40.50 per share, or $4,050. It's important because when you sell, you own taxes only on any gains you've realized over and above your cost basis in the shares.

With mutual funds, share prices in addition to any loads and redemption fees all factor into the cost basis of funds you own. However, if you pay a 6 percent load when you purchase a fund, this is already figured into your purchase price, so you don't need to add it again.

Suppose you sell shares and pay a 1 percent redemption fee. If you sell for $3,000, a 1 percent exit charge takes $30 out of your proceeds, leaving a net of $2,970, not $3,000. It can get complicated with mutual funds, particularly if you don't buy round lots, like 100 shares.

If you reinvest dividends and capital gains, count them when computing your cost basis. Reinvesting a taxable distribution is the same as putting new money into the fund. Forget to include these distributions in your cost basis, and you can wind up paying too much tax.

For the most part, investors and their tax advisers get little help from mutual fund companies when calculating the cost basis of an investment. Some companies are starting to provide average cost data, but most don't. You'll have to figure out your cost basis from your original transaction records. If you don't have accurate or complete records, your fund companies might help you by providing copies of past statements, occasionally charging a nominal fee.

It's easiest to compute your cost basis when you sell all your shares in a mutual fund account. Simply add up all the money you invested either directly or through dividend reinvestment, then subtract this cost from the proceeds of the sale to produce your gain or loss.

These calculations become more complicated if you've conducted more frequent transactions. For example, if you've held some shares in the account for more than one year, and others for less than a year, some profits will be taxable at one rate, some at another. Report this information on Schedule D of your federal tax return.

Table 6-2

Calculating Taxable Gains and Losses

On October 25, 1990, the net asset value, or per-share price, is $10.25. The total value of your holdings is $6,427.04. You are thinking about selling some of your shares in the fund. There are several ways to compute the tax consequences and minimize the tax bite.

Date of Purchase ▼	Amount ▼	Price/Share ▼	Shares Purchased ▼	Total Shares ▼
Feb. 15, 1989	$2,000.00	$10.00	200.000	200.000
June 2, 1989	1,000.00	11.75	85.106	285.106
Sept. 28, 1989	1,500.00	12.25	122.449	407.555
Dec. 15, 1989 Income distribution $0.15 per share and capital gains of $1 per share				
Reinvest income	6.13	10.90	5.608	413.163
Reinvest capital gains	407.00	10.90	37.931	450.554
May 10, 1990	1,000.00	10.40	96.154	546.708
July 6, 1990	1,000.00	12.45	80.321	627.029
Totals	$6,968.69	$11.11 (average)		

If you are selling all your shares, you can choose from these methods:

SINGLE-CATEGORY: Take the average cost of your shares, $11.11, and deduct the $10.25 current share price. That's an average loss of $0.86 per share. If all the shares have been held either long-term (more than a year) or short-term (less than a year) the loss would be 627.029 times $0.86, or $539.24. But in this case, 407.555 of the shares are long-term, and 219.474, short-term. Multiply each by $0.86, and you get a $350.50 long-term capital loss and a $188.75 short-term capital loss.

DOUBLE-CATEGORY: In the prior method, you calculate an average cost and apply it equally to long-term and short-term shares. In the double-category method, you calculate one average cost for the long-term shares and a separate average cost for the short-term shares. The 407.555 long-term shares cost $4,500, for an average cost of $11.04. These shares now show a $0.79 per share loss, for a total long-term loss of $321.97. The 219.474 short-term shares have an average cost of $11.25, and show a $1 per share loss. The total short-term loss is therefore $219.47.

If you are selling some but not all the shares, choose from these methods:

AVERAGE COST: Using the single-category method to redeem $3,000, you end up selling 292.683 shares at a loss of $0.86 each, for a long-term loss of $251.71. It's a long-term loss because the rules say that the oldest shares come out first.

SPECIFIC SHARES: In this method, you direct the fund to sell the costliest shares, those bought on June 2 and Sept. 28 of 1989 and July 6, 1990. The June 2 shares are now worth $872.34, for a loss of $127.66; the Sept. 28 shares, $1,255.10, for a loss of $244.90. Both are long-term losses. The July 6 shares purchased for $1,000 are worth $823.29, for a short-term loss of $176.71. Total redemptions are therefore about $2,951 with $549 in tax-deductible losses.

FIRST-IN, FIRST-OUT: If you don't tell your mutual fund company which shares to sell, the IRS will assume the oldest shares are sold first. As shown above, the first 200 shares have a cost basis of $10 each. If you sell those shares at $10.25, you have a taxable gain of $0.25 a share, or $50, even though your total investment is in the red. This is the least desirable method.

You'll want to calculate separate cost bases for your long-term shares and your short-term shares. It's a little extra work but can save you money by limiting the tax rate on your long-term profits to 28 percent. If you have gains, most likely the biggest ones are in the shares held long-term, so you'll want to allocate most of the gains there. If you simply calculate average costs per share, you'll put more of the gain on the short-term shares, resulting in a bigger tax bite.

The tax situation gets stickier if you sell some but not all your shares. Look at table 9.3. Suppose that on October 25 the fund's NAV is $10.25, your average cost is $11.11 per share, and you're considering selling some shares. You think you have a taxable loss of $0.86 per share—but that's only if you liquidate the entire account. If you sell only some shares and don't calculate your gains and losses by the proper method, the IRS will assume the first shares in are the first shares out.

Let's assume you ask the fund for a $2,000 redemption. That would result in the sale of 195.122 shares ($2,000 divided by $10.25). The IRS would assume those shares were from the first 200 shares you bought on February 15, 1989, at $10 per share. Though you have a loss on the entire investment, selling those shares even at October 25's depressed price would result in a taxable gain.

Fortunately, you can sell shares in a way that generates a tax-deductible loss. Go back to your average cost per share, $11.11. You can use the single- or double-category methods to calculate the tax liability on partial redemptions. (Remember to note your method on your tax return.) Sell $2,000 worth of shares by the single-category method and you get a tax loss of $168.

The specific-shares method (as previously described) is perhaps the best approach, although it takes some planning. You must designate in writing which shares are to be sold, and do so in advance of the transaction. This method enables you to pinpoint the highest-cost shares, in this case the ones you purchased June 2 and September 28, 1989, and July 6, 1990. These share prices were higher than today's NAV. By selling these shares, you can redeem $2,951 and still claim a tax-deductible loss of $549. Don't forget that with the specific-shares method—as with all the options—once you choose to redeem shares in a fund this way, all future redemptions must use the same method.

Investors using the single- or double-category methods to compute taxes should attach a note to their tax returns indicating so. Those using first-in, first-out or the specific-shares methods need not do so but should maintain their records in case of an audit. Keep in mind that rules change from time to time, so consult with your accountant or tax adviser before you do anything. It's also a good idea to get a free copy of Publication No. 564, "Mutual Fund Distributions," from the Internal Revenue Service.

Tax-Deferred Investing

IRAs

Mutual fund companies make great places to open Individual Retirement Accounts (IRAs) and other retirement accounts. Nearly 3 out of every 10 dollars presently in IRAs are invested in mutual funds, according to the Investment Company Institute. That's more than are invested with banks, savings and loans, or insurance companies. (Remember, though, that mutual fund investments are not insured.)

The mutual fund companies offer professional management, diversification, and a tendency toward long-term

investing. Mutual fund managers love retirement dollars, since the money tends to stay in place and generate fees for years. Most fund management companies will accept smaller opening minimums for IRAs, will shower you with plenty of literature on IRAs and the like, and provide specialists to explain the finer, more technical aspects of their investment programs. Fidelity Investments will even waive sales charges on many of its equity funds for IRA accounts.

In turn, IRA investors are fond of mutual funds, mainly because they provide an enormous variety of investment options. The only mutual funds that aren't good IRA investments are tax-exempt funds, since the interest is already free from taxation and is therefore lower than taxable interest would be.

If you don't already have an IRA, consider opening one. An IRA helps you save money for retirement, and produces tax savings, too. Taxpayers who qualify (more about that later) can salt away up to $2,000 a year—tax deferred. That is, you deduct the $2,000 from your adjusted gross income before figuring your income tax. What's more, your earnings in your IRA are not taxed until you withdraw them.

Taxpayers may start withdrawing from their IRAs when they are 59 1/2 years old, and must start withdrawals by age 70 1/2. The plans are so popular that IRAs already contain more than $725 billion, even after the 1986 federal tax reforms which cut back on IRA eligibility and cut tax rates. Check with your tax adviser to see if you're eligible for an IRA, and, if so, consider making your full contribution every year.

Wherever your IRA is presently located, you can move the funds to a mutual fund company with no penalty or loss of interest (this is called a "rollover"). If you withdraw a certificate of deposit before maturity, however, you may owe a penalty to the bank. Simply ask the mutual fund company to send you the necessary documents, fill them out, and send them in.

Most tax-deferred retirement accounts, including those with mutual fund companies, now carry an annual IRA "custodial" or "maintenance" fee. The fee, which takes care of the additional paperwork of an IRA, is typically $10 to $15 per year, but competition for the retirement accounts is so keen that many funds are starting to waive custodial fees for accounts over a certain size—say, $5,000 or $10,000. The mutual fund company will probably send a bill for the annual fee. If you don't pay by the due date, they'll deduct it from your account. Make plans to pay these fees separately, not out of the retirement account, since contributions to IRAs are strictly limited and the money removed will not be there to earn tax-deferred interest during the remaining life of the account.

Investors who are scheduled to receive their pension benefits in a lump-sum distribution because they're either retiring or changing jobs should be careful. Unless the money is transferred directly from their employer's pension plan into an IRA or other qualified retirement plan, the distribution will be subject to a 20 percent withholding tax. Those hit with the special tax then have 60 days to roll over the money into a qualified retirement account—or face additional taxes, including a 10 percent penalty for persons less than $59^{1}/_{2}$ years old.

If you need help with a rollover, the mutual fund company to which you're sending the money will gladly walk you through the process.

Keogh Plans

IRAs constitute just one of the retirement programs offered by mutual fund companies. They also hold about one-third of the money invested in retirement plans by the self-employed. Commonly known as Keogh plans, these are far more generous than IRAs, allowing self-employed investors to deduct as much as 25 percent of their income, up to $30,000, from their current year's taxes. These accounts are also far more complicated than IRAs, and get even trickier when the self-employed person has employees, who must also be covered by the plan.

There are several varieties of Keoghs. The program that allows the largest contribution (and highest

A smart way to tax defer your money is in a retirement fund such as an IRA or Keogh plan.

deduction) is the least flexible, and requires the same contribution every year. There's also the Simplified Employee Pension-Individual Retirement Account, otherwise known as a SEP or SEP-IRA. With these programs, the maximum contribution is generally $30,000, or 15 percent of annual compensation, whichever is less.

Because of the complexities of Keogh plans, you should consult an accountant or tax adviser before opening one of these accounts.

401(k) Plans

Mutual funds also offer the increasingly popular 401(k) plan. One of the features that makes 401(k)s different from conventional corporate pension plans is that the employee selects how the money is invested. That's why mutual funds make great places to keep 401(k) plan funds, although not every fund in every fund family is suitable.

Unfortunately you cannot start a 401(k) program for yourself; your employer must be the one to do it.

Mutual funds can also service 403(b) plans, which are like 401(k) plans but are exclusively for employees of certain charitable organizations or public school systems.

In both these plans, an employee can choose to place up to 10 percent of his or her pretax income (subject to an annually adjusted limit) in the plan's account, reducing that year's taxable income and thus cutting the tax bill. In addition, employers often "match" these employee contributions either in part or in full. The earnings of the 401(k) account are tax deferred, as with an IRA or Keogh plan, until the money is withdrawn at retirement.

Variable Annuities

Imagine owning a mutual fund that pays interest, dividends, and capital gains, all tax deferred. You can. It's called a variable annuity, one of the most interesting financial products on the market today. Most major mutual fund companies offer variable annuities or manage variable annuity investments for insurance companies. Like other retirement vehicles, the variable annuity carries the usual limitations on withdrawals before retirement age, and so forth.

The prime customers for variable annuities are mutual fund investors within 20 years of retirement who have assets to leave in place so as to benefit from tax deferrals on their

investment income. Many baby-boomers already fit this description, and more will every year.

The variable annuity sounds a lot like an IRA or a 401(k) plan, but it has several critical differences. First, contributions to it are not tax deductible. Second, there's no limit on what you can put in. Third, the costs of a variable annuity are higher than comparable mutual funds. For example, portfolio management expenses tend to be higher than for comparable mutual funds since the annuity funds are usually smaller. In addition, there's an annuity charge or "wrapper," which pays for a guarantee provided by an insurance company. The guarantee, which on average costs 1.27 percent per year, assures the investor's heirs that while the annuity contract is in force, it will be worth at least as much as the investor has contributed. (This is why variable annuities can be offered only by life insurance companies.) Finally, the investor who cashes out before retirement may pay a load, or a redemption charge, as high as 10 percent—and that's *before* any tax consequences. Thus, it's not advisable to invest in these annuities unless you're 99 percent sure you won't need the money for decades.

The insurance feature would come in handy for the heirs of someone who invests in a variable annuity holding, say, equity funds, and dies when the market is down and the investment has lost money. As a practical matter, however, the insurance is only worthwhile in the first few years of the annuity. After all, if the annuity is worth less than the contributions after 10 or 20 years, you chose the wrong investment. Unfortunately, annuity buyers can't elect to waive this guarantee—or its cost. It's the distinguishing feature of an annuity—essentially a life insurance policy that allows excess contributions to build up on a tax-deferred basis.

Some annuities now have a "step-up" provision that keeps raising the guaranteed death benefit. But that isn't free, either. The variable annuities look—and behave—much like mutual funds, but the terminology is different. There are no fund shares in a variable annuity; instead, the worth of the investment is tracked in "accumulation unit value," which, for practical purposes, is the same thing. A mutual fund available for investment with the money you've put into a variable annuity is a "subaccount." The average variable annuity has seven subaccount options.

Annuity funds are categorized much like conventional funds—growth, growth-and-income, balanced, government bond, and so forth. Most variable annuities also have a "fixed" account option, much like a bank certificate of deposit. However, there are no municipal bond annuity funds, since the income is already tax free.

Unlike conventional mutual funds, the majority of variable annuity assets are in equity-oriented subaccounts—mainly growth, growth-and-income, and balanced funds. This suggests annuity buyers really do have a long-term perspective.

Because fees for annuities can be much higher than for conventional mutual funds, some financial planners believe variable annuities are not really cost effective, particularly when cashed in early. Many are often sold as tax shelters, since the earnings of these subaccount investments are not taxed until withdrawal. These annuities, then, are best used as long-term savings vehicles. A study by analysts at Morningstar, Inc., concluded that a variable annuity works best for investors who stick with it for the long haul. Their higher expenses put annuities at a short-term disadvantage, compared with conventional mutual funds.

Consider, for example, an investor with a combined income tax rate of 37.4 percent. She invests in a variable annuity, which has an average annuity charge of 1.27 percent and a surrender charge of 6 percent. Let's assume the proceeds are taxed at a lower rate, 21.4 percent, during the "distribution" phase after retirement. If the annuity earns an average return of 6 percent per year, it takes 13 years before the tax-deferred annuity outperforms the totally taxable mutual fund. At 7 percent, the break-even year (when the two funds equal out) is Year 7, and afterward the annuity is the better choice. At 10 percent, which is considered the average long-term return from investing in equities, the annuity breaks even after Year 6.

These results are very sensitive to the annuity's fees and charges. For example, select an annuity that charges only 0.55 percent (the lowest in Morningstar's variable annuity database), and the trial run with a 7 percent average annual return breaks even in just five years, and the 10 percent trial breaks even in four. Eliminate the sales charge, too, and the annuity surpasses the regular account in just two years.

Be aware, however, that these examples assume the investor pays a lower tax rate when he or she starts withdrawing funds from the annuity. If there's enough income to remain in the top tax bracket after retirement, it takes 10 years for the annuity to break even with a regular account at a 7 percent annual rate of return, and 5 years to break even at a 10 percent rate. Even with a 1.5 percent annuity charge and no surrender charge, the annuity is a poor choice for the high-bracket investor: It takes 42 years to break even with a regular account at 7 percent, and 17 years at 10 percent.

Annuities are often sold to the wealthy as tax shelters, but they don't necessarily work out all that well. Suppose an investor chooses the variable annuity with the lowest annuity charges and no surrender charges. But if he or she withdraws the money prior to age 59 1/2, the funds are subject to a 10 percent penalty (that's U.S. tax law, not the annuity's). In this case, it takes 19 years at a 7 percent rate of return to break even with a regular account, and 12 years at 10 percent.

Before choosing to invest in a mutual fund variable annuity, compare the fund to a similar, taxable mutual fund. The higher charges and loss of financial flexibility may convince you not to go ahead, particularly if you want a maximum-growth or small-company fund. Most of these aggressive funds don't earn many dividends, and they rarely distribute capital gains.

If you're thinking of a government bond fund, municipal bond funds are a better buy: equally tax exempt, free of annuity charges, and totally without restrictions on withdrawals.

Conclusion

As you've seen throughout this book, mutual funds are one of the most exciting and potentially lucrative investment vehicles presently available. Whether you're going primarily for stability and safety, growth, income, or any combination of these, and whether you're interested in profiting from the broad, international economy, a particular region or nation, or only a small segment of worldwide economic activity, there's almost certainly a mutual fund tailormade to help you do it.

In this book we've given you a guided tour of the world of mutual funds, including detailed information on how they're classified and categorized, what types exist, how various types of funds operate, and how to evaluate which ones might be best for you. We've covered how to select a sound mutual fund, how to make the actual investment, what to do with dividends and interest you receive, and how to manage and monitor your entire mutual fund investment portfolio for maximum results over the long term.

But, of course, we can't actually *make* your mutual fund investments for you. It's up to *you* to take the information we've supplied and make good use of it—to develop an investment plan, to fund and implement it, and to monitor your resulting portfolio and the investment environment to make sure each of your funds keep performing as you desire.

As we've already recommended, you needn't jump into this type of investing with all your money in the very first week. It's far better to move gradually. Depending on how skillful you feel about making investments and how confident you are that you're making the right decisions, you can begin with anything from 1 percent to 20 percent of your total net worth.

Most people begin with a small- to medium-sized initial purchase of a single mutual fund—perhaps only a few thousand dollars or less—and then steadily add to this initial amount over subsequent weeks, months, and years as they let the power of compound interest help them build up a significant nest egg.

Another approach is to begin shifting your existing investments—whether CDs, stocks, or bonds—into equivalent mutual fund vehicles. That is, you can gradually sell your growth stocks and put the money into growth funds, sell your bonds and move the proceeds into bond funds, and switch your bank CDs into money-market mutual fund accounts, in accordance with the principles and practices we've outlined here.

In doing all this, of course, keep in mind what you've learned about mutual fund commissions, or "loads," and particularly the subtle differences and differing impacts between front-end loads, back-end loads, low-loads, and hidden loads. Also, remember that owning a bond will ultimately bring you to its maturity date, while owning a bond fund will not!

Although the world of mutual funds is vast and constantly changing, you've already received a comprehensive education in the basics. From here, you can go on to learn more through self-study about anything that interests you in the mutual fund world. You know the right people to deal with, the right questions to ask, and the right information to compare and contrast in making your mutual fund investment decisions.

Armed with the information in this book, and your own investment savvy, you can begin to make full use of the wonderful features of mutual funds—including the professional fund management, the selective investment opportunities, and both the automatic and intentional portfolio diversification funds can bring you—and begin to generate the kind of attractive and secure investment results that you previously could only dream about.

Index

P

R

S

T

U

V

W

Y

Z

Credits

Photos

All photos provided by The Image Bank, Northwest. **vi** Stephen Manks. **1** Michael Going. **4** C Van der Lende. **7** Charles Marsh. **9** Kay Chernush. **14** Gary Craelle. **15** Chuck Place. **16** Real Life. **17** Patti McConville. **19** G & V Chapman. **23** Murray Alcosser. **27** Salem Krieger. **33** William Lombardo. **35** L D Gordon. **37** Andrea Pistolesi. **39** Michel Tcherevkoff. **41** Nishi. **42** Peter Hendrie. **44** Stephen Marks. **47** Harold Sund. **50** Jeff Smith. **55** Alan Becker. **61** Yellow Dog Productions. **66** Kaz Mori. **69** Benn Mitchell. **70** Steve Niedorf. **72** L D Gordon. **75** BFI. **76** Yellow Dog Productions. **77** Ken Scallon. **78** Louis H. Jawitz. **79** James Noel Smith. **80** Curt Doty. **81** L D Gordon. **89** Jay Brousseau. **101** L D Gordon. **103** Tom Klare. **108** L D Gordon. **111** Michael Melford. **112** Kaz Mori. **113** Real Life. **114** L D Gordon. **117** L D Gordon.

Tables and Graphs

Data for tables and charts provided as follows:
2 Investment Company Institute, Strategic Insight. **6** Business Week. **10, 11, 12** Morningstar Inc. **20** T. Rowe Price Associates. **21** Business Week. **24 top, 24 bottom, 26, 28, 29, 30, 31** Morningstar Inc. **34** *IBC's Money Market Insight.* **39 top, 39 bottom, 46, 48, 51 top, 51 bottom** Morningstar Inc. **58** Strategic Insight. **71** Business Week. **82** Morningstar Inc. **83** Business Week. **86** Twentieth Century Investors, Business Week. **87** *Hulbert Financial Digest*, Morningstar Inc. **92, 95** Business Week. **107** Business Week, Morningstar Inc. **109** Business Week.